WOMEN'S RESILIENCE IN MONGOLIA

HOW LAWS AND POLICIES PROMOTE GENDER EQUALITY IN CLIMATE CHANGE AND DISASTER RISK MANAGEMENT

JUNE 2022

ASIAN DEVELOPMENT BANK

ADB

© 2022 Asian Development Bank
6 ADB Avenue, Mandaluyong City, 1550 Metro Manila, Philippines
Tel +63 2 8632 4444; Fax +63 2 8636 2444
www.adb.org

Some rights reserved. Published in 2022.

ISBN 978-92-9269-582-8 (print); 978-92-9269-583-5 (electronic); 978-92-9269-584-2 (ebook)
Publication Stock No. TCS220253-2
DOI: http://dx.doi.org/10.22617/TCS220253-2

Note:
In this publication, "$" refers to United States dollars.

Cover design by Cleone Baradas.

On the cover, a Mongolian woman poses in front of her gher, or residence. As climate change increased the occurrence of freezing weather events, i.e., *dzuds*, nomadic herders have been losing livestock, and as a result, have to move to urban areas seeking alternative livelihoods and income opportunities.

Contents

Tables, Figures, and Boxes

Foreword

The impact of climate change and disasters is contingent on various socioeconomic factors as well as country laws, policies, and decisions by policymakers. Gender roles and social inequalities in access to resources, care responsibilities, and lower levels of education systematically disadvantage women and girls, rendering them more vulnerable to the impact of climate change and disasters. Numerous reports have revealed disproportionately higher mortality rates among women and girls during disasters, further highlighting that this area of work requires closer attention from governments and development partners.*

The Asian Development Bank (ADB) works with developing member country stakeholders with a shared vision to strengthen approaches to address climate change and improve disaster resilience through investments in water supply, sanitation, irrigation, flood control, transport, and energy, as well as to increase knowledge sharing and cooperation with partners in the region. It is understood that a "business as usual" approach no longer works for tackling increasingly complex problems in Asia and the Pacific. A holistic and truly cross sector and thematic approach is needed, with gender equality being a central consideration for the effectiveness and sustainability of climate change and disaster risk management (CCDRM) actions.

ADB has been promoting "integrated approaches" and working to mainstream gender equality and women's empowerment in operations to support developing member countries in their efforts to become resilient to climate change and disasters. Improved gender equality and women's empowerment turn into positive benefits for many other development goals and targets. The ADB Strategy 2030 Operational Plan for Priority Two on *Accelerating Gender Equality* outlines a clear vision of gender equality as an effective means for achieving sustainable and inclusive growth, including in the area of climate and disaster resiliency.

This Mongolia country report is part of a series of publications that applies the *National Good Practice Framework* presented in the regional report *Gender-Inclusive Legislative Framework and Laws to Strengthen Women's Resilience to Climate Change and Disasters*, to explore the extent of integration of gender considerations in CCDRM laws, policies and plans in Fiji, the Lao People's Democratic Republic (Lao PDR), and Mongolia. It was prepared under a regional knowledge and support technical assistance project on *Strengthening Women's Resilience to Climate Change and Disaster Risk in Asia and the Pacific*. The project specifically aims to increase the capacity of these three countries to develop and advance gender responsive CCDRM national and sector policies and laws. It also contributes to the wider thrust of the ADB Gender Equality Thematic Group to promote national legislation that supports women's resilience through gender inclusive approaches to CCDRM.

---

* S. Brown et al. 2019. Gender and Age Inequality of Disaster Risk: *Research Paper*. UNICEF and UN Women.

This report is important as ADB commitments are turned into actions. In light of the increasing complexity of climate and disaster risk challenges in the Asia and Pacific region, it adds to the understanding of gaps, as well as good practices in CCDRM laws and policies, and provides recommendations for moving forward. This report should serve as valuable input to support government agencies and policymakers in Mongolia to make country laws and policies gender-responsive and supportive to women's resilience to climate change and disasters.

Samantha Hung
Chief of Gender Equality Thematic Group
Sustainable Development and Climate Change Department
Asian Development Bank

Acknowledgments

This report is based on work undertaken under the Asian Development Bank (ADB) Technical Assistance (TA) 9348-REG: *Strengthening Women's Resilience to Climate Change and Disaster Risk in Asia and the Pacific*. Overall, the regional project objective is to strengthen the capacity of policymakers in three countries: Fiji, the Lao People's Democratic Republic (Lao PDR) and Mongolia, and to make climate change and disaster risk management (DRM) policies, strategies, or financing more gender-responsive. This Mongolia country report on climate change and DRM law and policy frameworks is one element of the project, and similar reports have been prepared for Fiji and Lao PDR.

The report was prepared under the overall guidance of Malika Shagazatova (social development specialist) and Zonibel Woods (senior social development specialist) of the ADB Sustainable Development and Climate Change Department (SDCC). Support and contributions were provided by Alih Faisal Pimentel Abdul (TA coordinator), Erdenechimeg Tserendorj (national gender consultant), Ma. Celia A. Guzon (senior operations assistant), and Tsolmon Begzsuren (senior social development officer) of the ADB Mongolia Resident Mission. Consultants Robyn Layton (gender and law expert) and Mary Picard, (climate change and disaster risk management/environmental law expert) drafted the report. The report was edited by Amy Reggers, gender and climate change consultant.

Special thanks to Samantha Hung, chief of gender equality thematic group, SDCC; and Sonomi Tanaka, country director, Lao People's Democratic Republic and former chief of gender equity thematic group, SDCC, for their overall support and guidance in the implementation of the TA.

The report benefited significantly from comments by Enkhbayar Tumur-Ulzii, National Committee on Gender Equality (NCGE) Secretary and Chief of the NCGE Secretariat of Mongolia, as well as national gender experts Onon Byambasuren and Solongo Sharkhuu.

Special thanks for the contributions of participants in two national workshops in Mongolia.

Abbreviations

ADB	Asian Development Bank
CEACR	ILO Committee of Experts on the Application of Conventions and Recommendations
CEDAW	Convention on the Elimination of All Forms of Discrimination Against Women
DRM	Disaster Risk Management
DRR	Disaster Risk Reduction
EIA Law	Law on Environmental Impact Assessments
GHG	greenhouse gas
GIZ	Deutsche Gesellschaft für Internationale Zusammenarbeit (German International Development Agency)
ILO	International Labour Organization
LCDV	Law to Combat Domestic Violence
LEP	Law on Environmental Protection
LPGE	Law on Promotion of Gender Equality
MET	Ministry of Environment and Tourism
NAPCC	National Action Programme on Climate Change
NCGE	National Committee on Gender Equality
NDC	Nationally Determined Contribution
NEMA	National Emergency Management Agency
NGDP	National Green Development Policy
NHRC	National Human Rights Commission
NPGE	National Programme on Gender Equality
NSO	National Statistics Office
SDG	Sustainable Development Goal
UNFCCC	United Nations Framework Convention on Climate Change
UNFPA	United Nations Population Fund
WHO	World Health Organization

Executive Summary

Mongolia has a strong capacity for sustainable development due to its highly skilled, educated, and resilient population and a wealth of natural resources. It also faces significant sustainability and environmental challenges that are amplified by climate change. The harsh climate, substantial natural hazards, and unique geography are compounded by rapid growth that relies on coal-based energy and the dominant economic sectors of mining and pastoralism that both also contribute to ecological challenges. Coal remains the primary energy source and energy demand is increasing with economic and population growth. Air pollution has become a major issue in the growing city of Ulaanbaatar, with increasing vehicle traffic and nearby coal-fired power stations that contribute to both greenhouse gas (GHG) emissions and pollutants. This creates tension between climate change commitments under the Paris Agreement, economic growth targets, and significant social and health concerns, particularly for women and children.

Pastoralism still provides the livelihood of 40% of the population, and the industry is highly vulnerable to natural hazards, especially climate extremes and desertification. Mongolia is already one of the most arid countries in the world, with over 90% of the territory classified as arid to moisture deficient, which is exacerbated by deforestation and land degradation. Climate change adds another layer to sustainability issues. Since 1950, average mean temperatures have increased three times faster than the global average. Rather than resulting in a generally milder climate, the magnitude and frequency of climatic hazards appear to be increasing, especially summer droughts leading to winter *dzuds* (a sudden freezing event). Climate projections for Mongolia indicate harsher winter conditions for pastoralists due to heavier winter snow and more *dzud* events, along with poorer quality summer pasture, and a reduction in wheat yields for crop farmers. The resulting challenges for Mongolia include rural impoverishment, rapid urbanization, and changes in education and work opportunities that also impact family relations and work-related gender roles. These challenges can negatively impact the overall gender equality situation.

The successes of Mongolia in progressing gender equality in health and education are noteworthy; yet the Global Gender Gap Report 2020 found that overall, the ranking of Mongoila has fallen from its 2016 indices in three out of the four areas.[a] Particular areas of concern are political empowerment, and economic participation and opportunity. There are also serious concerns about the persistence of gender-based violence. These key areas of socioeconomic development are likely to be exacerbated further with the increasing rise in climate and disaster related risks. Therefore—important alongside the challenges of combating disaster and climate impacts—there is a need for women and men to move forward with increased equality of outcomes. This requires a focus on improving gender equality in key socioeconomic areas, as well as specific attention to the way disasters and climate change impact women and men differently in Mongolia, and how laws and policy responses can be more gender responsive.

The purpose of this report was to conduct a gender analysis of the national legal and policy frameworks of Mongolia to determine whether laws, policies, and strategies consider gender inequalities as they relate to climate and disaster risk and contribute to strengthening women's resilience. The laws of a country set the legal framework and provide the foundation to regulate a sector and guarantee fundamental rights, and policies should further amplify

---

a   World Economic Forum. 2019. *Global Gender Gap Report 2020*. Geneva.

legal provisions and implement legislative guarantees. For the analysis in this report, a National Good Practice Legislative Framework has been developed. The framework draws on (i) the Committee on the Elimination of Discrimination Against Women (CEDAW Committee) General Recommendation No. 37 on the *Gender-related dimensions of disaster risk reduction in the context of climate change* (CEDAW GR37); and (ii) a newly published report on best practice legal frameworks in Asia and the Pacific, which assists in selecting laws and policies related to the national approach to gender equality, climate, and disaster risks as well as socioeconomic development to be gender analyzed.[b] The analysis of the selected laws and policies inform an assessment of the extent to which equality and discrimination concepts are explicit in laws and policies and how this affects women's resilience to climate and disaster risks. The report refers to gender and gender-responsiveness as much as possible rather than to women only. The report methodology included secondary data collection and analysis, supported by a country mission, stakeholder interviews, and national workshops.

Results of the analysis found a high commitment to addressing gender equality and prohibiting discrimination; these concepts—as well as international law on the topic—are imported into the Constitution of Mongolia, the Law on the Promotion of Gender Equality (LPGE)—which is considered global best practice,—and the National Programme on Gender Equality (NPGE). The LPGE has also generated the development of 11 gender responsive sector strategies. For example, these include the Population, Labor and Social Protection Sector Strategy; the Food, Agriculture, and Light Industry Sector Strategy; and—particularly relevant to this report—the Environmental Sector Strategy; all of which are explicit in the promotion of gender equality and nondiscrimination.

Despite these achievements, the analysis reveals that there is a distinct lack of commitment to equality and nondiscrimination in key disaster risk management, environment, and climate change laws and policies. Disaster risk management and environmental laws rely on the inclusion of the Constitution and make no explicit mention of the LPGE or gender equality. Notable exceptions are the National Action Programme on Climate Change (NAPCC) 2011—which includes gender equality as an implementation principle and mentions the need to promote the representation of women in international and regional forums,—and the Environment Sector Gender Strategy. Similar findings from a close analysis of energy laws and policies reveal no integration of equality and non-discrimination principles and no mention of the gender dimensions of energy considered in laws or policies related to energy.

In addition to sector-specific laws and policies, several laws governing socioeconomic areas which can contribute to building women's resilience to climate change and disaster risk were analyzed. The report focuses on three areas (i) combating gender-based violence (GBV), (ii) improving women's access to assets, and (iii) improving access by women to decent work. Findings reveal the Mongolia Law to Combat Domestic Violence is a best practice law. However, concerns exist around gender responsive implementation of this law, including insufficient access to shelters and services for women during normal times. This issue becomes even more critical in the context of disaster risk management.

In terms of women's access to assets, the Civil Code and Family Law regard all assets and properties of marriage and family as joint property and declare an equal right to inheritance.[c] However, research on actual practice shows that men are twice as likely as women to be documented (51% men versus 27% women), reported dwelling owners (60% men versus 33% women), or livestock related property owners (33% men versus 18% women) in Mongolia.[d] When it comes to agricultural land, a very low rate of both documented (6% men versus 1% women) and reported

[b]   Asian Development Bank (ADB). 2021. *Gender-Inclusive Legislative Framework and Laws to Strengthen Women's Resilience to Climate Change and Disaster Risk*. Manila.

[c]   The World Bank. 2021. *Women, Business and Law*. The report assessed the property rights in Mongolian laws by following four indicators and concluded that law provides equal rights to possess, use and dispose joint properties. (i) Equality in Property rights? Yes. Civil Code 127.2 and 128.1; (ii) Equal rights of inheritance of the parents' property? Yes. Civil Code 520.1.1; (iii) Equal rights of inheritance of spouse's property? Yes. Civil Code 520.1.1; and (iv) Equal rights of managing family property by spouses? Yes. Civil Code 128.1.

[d]   Government of Mongolia, National Statistics Office (NSO). 2018. *Measuring Asset Ownership and Entrepreneurship from a Gender Perspective: Pilot Study Report* (in original language). Ulaanbaatar.

(8% men versus 2% women) possession for both men and women exists.[e] Awareness about alienation rights (the right to sell or bequeath) to core assets slightly differs between men (97%) and women (90%) in Mongolia. Around 10% of female owners in Mongolia reported that they do not have the right to sell their owned dwelling units.[f]

Given the disparities in land registration between women and men—and the important role land plays in pastoralism in the country—gender responsive laws and policies in this area are crucial. The Law on Pastureland Usage has not yet passed Parliament; therefore this is regulated by the Law on Land and other legislations. The Law on Land includes provision 4.1.3 which states "to ensure fairness and equality in land ownership, possession and use," however there is no other mention of gender equality or nondiscrimination.[g] Finally, the analysis found several areas of concern regarding decent work for women that are not explicitly addressed by sector law or policy (some of these issues are identified in the LPGE), or that the laws perpetuate discrimination. These include workplace harassment, an increasing gender pay gap, and unequal retirement age for women and men.

In conclusion, the report finds that while the LPGE and the NPGE serve as a gender responsive framework for women's rights and development in Mongolia, sector laws and policies that affect women's resilience to climate change and disasters in Mongolia are not yet gender mainstreamed. There are two exceptions: (i) the NAPCC is classified as gender sensitive; and (ii) the Environmental Sector Gender Strategy stands out as the gender responsive policy that directly promotes strengthening women's resilience. Yet, without a suite of policy initiatives—as well as legislation to enforce commitments to gender equality—it is unclear how effective the NAPCC and the sector strategy alone will be in strengthening women's resilience to climate and disaster risks. The report includes a set of specific and general recommendations to address some of these gaps.

Specific Recommendations:

(i)   **Develop an Emergency Management Sector Gender Strategy** in the short term, to ensure protection and equality principles for disaster risk reduction are in place.

(ii) **Review the National Program of Community Participatory Disaster Risk Reduction (2015–2025)** at its mid-point from a gender perspective and advocate for the inclusion of specific gender equality targets and the promotion of gender inclusive approaches to community participation in DRR.

(iii) **Develop regulations under the Law on Environmental Protection and the Environmental Impact Assessment (EIA) Law** to increase the gender responsiveness of public participation in environmental policy.

(iv) **Develop an Energy Sector Gender-Responsive Policy** to identify key gender dimensions of the energy sector and include equality and on-discrimination principles in one of Mongolia's critical sectors.

General Recommendations:

(i)   **Collection and analysis of disaggregated data needs to be prioritized.**

(ii) **Increasing women's participation in environmental decision making is essential.**

(iii) **Consolidate a gender responsive approach to climate change and disaster risk.**

---

[e]   Government of Mongolia, NSO. 2018. *Asset Ownership and Entrepreneurship from a Gender Perspective Pilot Study Report* (in original language). Ulaanbaatar.

[f]   ADB. 2018. *Measuring Asset Ownership and Entrepreneurship from a Gender Perspective: Methodology and Results of Pilot Surveys in Georgia, Mongolia, and the Philippines.* Manila.

[g]   Government of Mongolia. 2002. *Law on Land 2002.* Ulaanbaatar.

1 Background

On the global scale, there is increasing political consensus that the transition to cleaner, more sustainable development includes not only increasing the number of women in climate and environment related decision making, but also promoting gender equality as part of climate action and disaster risk management (DRM). Gender equality and social inclusion are increasingly seen as essential to sustainable development and a just transition to a low-carbon climate future.

Key international treaties recommend or mandate the inclusion of gender equality indicators as part of the reporting obligations of State Parties and some treaty bodies are leading by example through gender action plans. Under the United Nations Framework Convention on Climate Change (UNFCCC), a gender action plan includes targets for increased representation and participation of women in UNFCCC processes, a gender balance goal at intergovernmental meetings, and guidance for State Parties in their efforts to integrate gender equality issues into their national commitments, reporting processes and plans. These efforts are translating into results: a 2020 gender analysis of Nationally Determined Contributions (NDCs) under the Paris Agreement demonstrates that 50% of updated NDCs have a reference to gender or women compared to only 33% in 2016, and several Parties that did not refer to gender in their 2016 submission now include references to gender, some in substantive ways. All of the new NDCs (countries that had not previously submitted any NDC) include a reference to women or gender.[1]

Similarly—within global disaster risk management efforts—the Sendai Framework for Disaster Risk Reduction 2015-2030, the Ha Noi Recommendations for Action on Gender and Disaster Risk Reduction, and the Ulaanbaatar Declaration of the 2018 Asian Ministerial Conference on Disaster Risk Reduction all recognize the importance of promoting the participation of women in decision making in disaster risk reduction (DRR) and ensuring gender-sensitive policies for disaster risk management. The Ulaanbaatar Declaration specifically called on all governments and stakeholders to:

> "Promote full and equal participation of women in leading, designing, and implementing gender-sensitive disaster risk reduction policies, plans and programmes, through joint efforts by public and private sector, supported by appropriate legal frameworks and allocation of necessary resources."[2]

The Committee for the Elimination of Discrimination Against Women (CEDAW Committee) is the treaty body of the long-standing Convention on the Elimination of All Forms of Discrimination Against Women (CEDAW Convention). It sets out in General Recommendation No. 37 the obligations of Member States on the gender-related dimensions of disaster risk reduction in the context of climate change (CEDAW GR37). This outlines the requirement for national policies and plans to address gender inequality, reduce disaster risk, and increase resilience to the adverse effects of climate change. The CEDAW Committee notes that the focus needs to go beyond climate change and disaster risk policies and plans to also include national socioeconomic and development plans.

---

1   Women's Environment and Development Organisation. 2020. *Gender Climate Tracker: Quick Analysis.*
2   Government of Mongolia, Asian Ministerial Conference on Disaster Risk Reduction. 2018. *Ulaanbaatar Declaration.* Ulaanbaatar. p. 2.

Despite growing recognition of the need to integrate gender equality and full and effective participation of women in climate change action and disaster risk management, a 2020 UN Women report notes that inconsistencies remain in national legislation, policies, and plans.[3] There remains a capacity gap in many countries to integrate their gender equality and women's empowerment commitments into climate change and disaster risk management legal frameworks, policies, and plans. These frameworks have a critical role in implementing these national commitments, however the adequacy of such frameworks concerning gender equality is yet to be comprehensively reviewed. This report focuses on Mongolia, and is part of a three-country series that includes Fiji and the and the Lao People's Democratic Republic. It contributes to addressing the information gap by providing the results of a gender analysis of national laws and policy frameworks to understand whether and how they include gender equality concepts and language to form a strong foundation for promoting women's resilience to climate change and disasters.

1.1   Introduction

Mongolia is facing significant weather-related disasters and the impacts of climate change. The country has already seen an average temperature increase of three times the global average.[4] Far from creating a gentler climate across the board, this appears to have generated greater weather extremes, blending climate impacts with phenomena that have led to disasters. In particular, hazards such as the sudden freezing weather events known as *dzuds*— as well as increasing drought and desertification—impact traditional pastoralist livelihoods and lead to rural impoverishment. This is accelerating migration to urban areas[5] which puts pressure on the social, economic, and physical infrastructure of Ulaanbaatar and other urban centers.[6]

Sudden disaster impacts are overwhelmingly negative, but the need to adapt to and mitigate climate change is a more mixed phenomenon that can also bring positive opportunities through the social changes it triggers. Mongolia is fortunate because it is a lower middle-income country with a strong capacity for sustainable development due to its highly skilled, educated, and resilient population and a wealth of natural resources.[7] It has a great potential for adaptation. A commitment to green technology has seen improvements to quality of life and prosperity with the introduction of solar panels in rural areas that were not on the grid (giving access to mobile phones; weather reports; bright light; and solar power for study, reading, work, and TV).[8] Agriculture adaptation to climate change has led some pastoralist families to pool their resources in new ways, reinforcing community and tradition,[9] and others to reduce animal stocks and prosper from small-scale tourism.[10] There are also future work opportunities in large-scale reforestation and renewable energy technologies, which are government priorities for climate mitigation[11] and adaptation.[12]

Important in the pursuit of climate adaptation and mitigation—as well as disaster risk management—is ensuring that both women and men are included, and that past gender inequality is addressed so that they can share equally in the benefits of risk-informed development. Gender inequalities in key socioeconomic areas in normal times can

[3]   H. Nguyen et al. 2020. *Review of Gender Responsiveness and Disability Inclusion in Disaster Risk Reduction in Asia and the Pacific.* Bangkok: UN Women.

[4]   United Nations Development Programme. 2019. *Mongolia Achieves a Milestone in National Adaptation Planning.* Press release. 20 March.

[5]   J. Neve. 2016. *Climate Change and Savage Winters Fuel Urban Migration in Mongolia.* International Organization for Migration (IOM). Press Release. 29 September.

[6]   IOM. 2018. *Mongolia: Internal Migration Study.* Ulaanbaatar.

[7]   World Bank Group. 2021. *Mongolia.*

[8]   World Bank. 2014. *Mongolia : Development Impacts of Solar-Powered Electricity Services. Asia Sustainable and Alternative Energy Program.* Washington, DC: World Bank. .

[9]   J. Pasotti. 2017. *How Mongolia's Nomads Are Adapting to Climate Change.* DW. 24 July.

[10]   United Nations Economic Social Commission on Asia and the Pacific and Government of Mongolia. 2018. *Sustainability Outlook of Mongolia.* Munkhiin Useg.

[11]   In terms of funded programming, see the Green Climate Fund. 2019. *Country Programme Mongolia.* March 19.

[12]   United Nations Development Programme. 2019. *Mongolia Achieves a Milestone in National Adaptation Planning.*

impact the ability of women to benefit from climate action and to build resilience.[13] In Mongolia, structural gender inequality and discrimination against women in several socioeconomic spheres—such as women's economic participation, women's political representation, and grave rights violations such as gender-based violence (GBV)—exist.. To address these issues and enable women to build resilience, gender equality and nondiscrimination principles need to be embedded in laws and policies and actively implemented in programs and activities, not only in those related to climate and disaster risks but in socioeconomic development more broadly.

In this report, key national laws and policies in Mongolia are analyzed to understand how they provide a legal foundation and explicit commitment to strengthening women's resilience to climate change and disasters. This is done by looking at the national commitments to promoting gender equality, analyzing climate and disaster risk management laws and policies—with a specific focus on the energy sector—and analysis of selected socioeconomic areas that directly relate to building women's resilience, including including GBV prevention, rights to access to land and assets, and decent work.

1.2 Purpose and Scope

Gender differences in the impacts of climate change and disasters are related to preexisting inequality and discrimination. Differentiated gender roles mean that hazards may impact women and men differently. In general, disasters exacerbate prior disadvantages, while climate change adaptation can provide new opportunities as well as potentially reinforce existing disadvantages. To minimize the adverse impacts of climate change and disasters and improve women's resilience to these risks, it is necessary to understand underlying gender inequality and discrimination against women.

The purpose of this report is to conduct a gender analysis of key elements of the national legal and policy frameworks of Mongolia to determine the extent to which laws, policies, and strategies consider gender equality, and contribute to strengthening women's resilience to climate change and disaster risks. The report begins by presenting a framework for selecting and analyzing relevant laws and policies. The framework draws on CEDAW GR37 and builds on a national framework approach developed in a regional ADB report on best practices in legislation.[14] A country profile is presented to set the context, including key climate hazards and a description of the situation for women in Mongolia with a focus on socioeconomic areas that impact resilience building. A gender analysis is then conducted on a range of laws and policies relevant to disaster risk management, climate change, the energy sector, and key areas of women's socioeconomic resilience. The report concludes with an analysis of the extent to which the laws and policies promote women's resilience and makes recommendations to enhance the inclusion of gender equality commitments in laws and policies to strengthen women's resilience to climate change and disasters.

The key aims of this report are to

(i)   develop a *National Good Practice Legislative Framework for Strengthening Women's Resilience to Climate Change and Disasters* which governments can use to analyze laws, policies, and institutions related to climate change and disaster risk management;

(ii)   apply the framework and present the analysis to the Government of Mongolia in light of the national context and international standards to determine how gender responsive laws and policies are; and

(iii)   make recommendations on how the government can enhance the commitment to gender equality through laws and policies that promote women's resilience through gender responsive climate change and disaster risk management.

---

[13]   C. Pross et al. 2020. *Climate change, gender equality and human rights in Asia: regional review and promising practices.* UN Women.

[14]   ADB. 2021. *Gender-Inclusive Legislative Framework and Laws to Strengthen Women's Resilience to Climate Change and Disaster Risk.* Manila.

1.3 A National Good Practice Legislative Framework for Strengthening Women's Resilience to Climate Change and Disasters

To achieve the first aim of this report, a *National Good Practice Legislative Framework for Strengthening Women's Resilience to Climate Change and Disasters* was developed. The framework draws on the Convention on the Elimination of all Forms of Discrimination Against Women's (CEDAW Convention) and CEDAW GR37. The CEDAW Convention is a binding international treaty that was adopted in 1979 by the UN General Assembly and is often described as an international bill of rights for women. Consisting of a preamble and 30 articles, it defines what constitutes discrimination against women and sets up an agenda for national action to end such discrimination. Mongolia is a party to the CEDAW Convention without any current reservations.

Given the global focus on climate change, disaster risk reduction, and the significant impact on human life and livelihood, the CEDAW Committee added CEDAW GR37 in 2018. CEDAW GR37 discusses how the different aspects of the CEDAW Convention apply to these risks and makes expert recommendations to State Parties on how to address each of them. It states: "the Committee has underlined that States Parties and other stakeholders have obligations to take concrete steps to address discrimination against women in the fields of disaster risk reduction and climate change through the adoption of targeted laws, policies, mitigation and adaptation strategies, budgets and other measures."[15]

CEDAW GR37 underscores the general principles of the CEDAW Convention applicable to climate change and disaster risk: substantive equality and nondiscrimination, participation and empowerment, and accountability and access to justice (footnote 23). It notes special measures—such as disaggregated data collection by sex, age, disability, ethnicity, geographical location and its use, policy coherence, capacity development, and alignment with extra-territorial obligations—that State Parties should prioritize in the pursuit of reducing disaster risk for women.[16] Overall, CEDAW GR37 outlines how an increase in women's resilience to climate change and disaster risks needs support from broader socioeconomic laws and policies as well as the realization of specific rights such as the right to live free from GBV, the right to work, social protection, and the right to health among others (footnote 24).

Building on the general principles of the CEDAW Convention, the specific areas of concern under CEDAW GR37 and the report on global good practice and international standards, Figure 1 presents the *National Good Practice Legislative Framework for Strengthening Women's Resilience to Climate Change and Disasters*.[17] When the framework is in place, the institutional mandates, policies, and strategies have a solid legal base. They in turn can support gender-responsive resource allocation decisions and the use of gender analysis and gender mainstreaming in the implementation of the laws and policies.

Section 2 of the report is structured according to the framework. Section 2.1 analyzes the Constitution of Mongolia and the national laws that promote gender equality and prohibit discrimination. Given the number of laws related to climate change and disaster risk, this thematic area has been divided and section 2.2 covers laws related to disaster risk management, while laws related to climate change and environmental management are reviewed in section 2.3. Given the significance of the energy sector to mitigation and the importance of energy to Mongolia overall, a gender analysis of laws related to energy is presented in section 2.4. Finally, national laws and policies that contribute to building women's socioeconomic resilience are analyzed and presented in section 2.5. It is noted that

---

[15] CEDAW. 2018. *General Recommendation No. 37 on Gender-Related Dimensions of Disaster Risk Reduction in the Context of Climate Change* (CEDAW/C/GC/37). para. 8. New York: CEDAW.

[16] This report adopts CEDAW's recommended minimum standards of disaggregated data. This suggests data be disaggregated by sex, age, disability, ethnicity, and geographical location as much as possible. The term "sex-disaggregated data" is used for brevity throughout this report.

[17] ADB. 2021. *Gender-Inclusive Legislative Framework and Laws to Strengthen Women's Resilience to Climate Change and Disaster Risk*. Manila.

Figure 1: A National Good Practice Legislative Framework for Strengthening Women's Resilience to Climate Change and Disasters

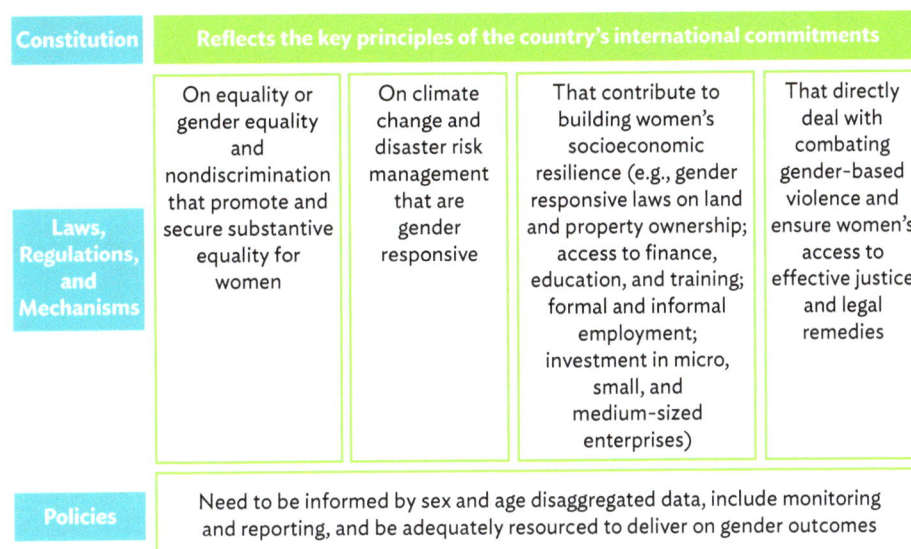

Constitution	Reflects the key principles of the country's international commitments			
Laws, Regulations, and Mechanisms	On equality or gender equality and nondiscrimination that promote and secure substantive equality for women	On climate change and disaster risk management that are gender responsive	That contribute to building women's socioeconomic resilience (e.g., gender responsive laws on land and property ownership; access to finance, education, and training; formal and informal employment; investment in micro, small, and medium-sized enterprises)	That directly deal with combating gender-based violence and ensure women's access to effective justice and legal remedies
Policies	Need to be informed by sex and age disaggregated data, include monitoring and reporting, and be adequately resourced to deliver on gender outcomes			

Source: ADB. 2021. *Gender-Inclusive Legislative Framework and Laws to Strengthen Women's Resilience to Climate Change and Disaster Risk*. Manila

the full spectrum of laws and policies as set out in the framework cannot be addressed in this report. However, some of these thematic issues are touched upon throughout the analysis.

1.4 Methodology

The primary methodology in preparing the report was desk-based research and gender analysis of selected laws and policies, supplemented by country consultations, national workshops, and feedback on a draft report. Using the framework developed, a selection of laws and policies from Mongolia were gender analyzed.

The gender analysis encompassed the following steps:

(i)   review the overall purpose of the law or policy;
(ii)   assess the relevance of the instrument to gender, its content, and its potential impact upon women, especially women's resilience;
(iii)   look at the language used and determine whether it makes distinctions based on sex, gender roles, or gender stereotypes;
(iv)   assess laws or policies on a continuum of gender integration from lowest to highest: gender negative, gender neutral, gender sensitive, gender-responsive, to gender positive and/or transformative. Then classify them into three main recurring categories: gender responsive, gender sensitive, or not yet gender mainstreamed, with some additional specific references to gender positive and/or transformative examples; and
(v)   make recommendations and/or highlight any good practices in the law or policy to enhance the commitment to gender equality through laws and policies that contribute to promoting women's resilience in climate change and disaster risks.

The purpose of classifying laws and policies on a continuum is to identify where gaps exist and where best practice examples can be highlighted. The continuum is adapted from the UN Women Training Centre,[18] and WHO 2012 Mainstreaming Gender in Health Adaptation to Climate Change Programmes.[19] This analysis applies a three-point scale (color coded throughout) using authoritative international terminology:

(i)   **Gender responsive (green):** Pays attention to specific needs of women and men and intentionally uses gender considerations to affect the design, implementation, and results of legislation, policies, and programs.[20]

(ii) **Gender sensitive (yellow):** Considers gender norms, roles, and relations taking into account sociocultural factors, but does not actively address gender inequalities.[21]

(iii) **Not yet gender mainstreamed (orange):** No attention to gender equality issues have been made, which may result in a gender neutral or a gender negative outcome.

It is important to note that where possible, the report refers to gender and gender-responsiveness as much as possible rather than to women only. This recognizes that laws, policies, programs, and actions affect both men and women and that sometimes gender roles can disadvantage women and girls and sometimes disadvantage men and boys, often in different ways. However, based on CEDAW GR37 and the gender-based vulnerabilities and risks to the realization of women's rights from climate and disaster risk, the report focuses specifically on women's resilience. This is in alignment with the pursuit of gender equality and empowerment of women and girls under Sustainable Development Goal 5 (SDG5) and was articulated in the *Asia-Pacific Declaration on Advancing Equality and the Women's Empowerment: Beijing+25 Review*.[22] Therefore, this report primarily addresses how laws, policies, and gender mainstreaming can enhance women's resilience to these risks in Mongolia.

1.5   Gender, Climate Change, and Disaster Profile of Mongolia

The following profile highlights key climate hazards and disaster risks in Mongolia and then presents the socioeconomic profile of women in the country as it relates to the identified risks.

Climate and disaster risk. Mongolia faces significant environmental management challenges that are amplified by climate change. The challenges arise from rapid growth, a harsh climate, its unique geography, substantial natural hazards, and the economic dominance of mining and pastoralism.[23] The average altitude of the country is 1,580 meters above sea level, and is therefore generally colder than other countries of the same latitude; around the capital city Ulaanbaatar, annual average temperatures range from −22°C to 17°C. There are six ecological zones, from the high mountain alpine systems in the north and east to the vast Gobi Desert in the south, which covers about 40% of the territory. There are four distinct seasons, with the driest months between November and March. Mongolia is one of the aridest countries in the world, with over 90% of the territory classified as arid to moisture deficient.

Mongolia is already experiencing the adverse effects of climate change (Table 1). Climate projections for Mongolia using a range of models indicate that continued global warming will increase winter temperatures and winter snow; that summer temperatures will not increase so much but summer rainfall will increase slightly. These changing

[18]   UN Women Training Centre. 2017. *Gender Equality Glossary.*
[19]   WHO. 2012. *Mainstreaming Gender in Health Adaptation to Climate Change Programmes.* Table 1. p. 10. Geneva.
[20]   UNICEF. 2017. *Gender Equality Glossary of Terms and Concepts.*
[21]   WHO. 2012. *Mainstreaming Gender in Health Adaptation to Climate Change Programmes.* Geneva.
[22]   Economic and Social Commission for Asia and the Pacific (ESCAP). 2019. *Asia-Pacific Declaration on Advancing Gender Equality and Women's Empowerment: Beijing +25 Review.* Prepared for the Asia-Pacific Ministerial Conference on the Beijing+25 Review. Beijing. 27–29 November.
[23]   ADB. 2017. *Inclusive and Sustainable Growth Assessment Mongolia 2017–2020.* Manila.

weather patterns are projected to cause harsher winter conditions for pastoralists and their grazing animals, along with poorer quality summer pasture, and a reduction in wheat yields.[24]

Table 1: An Overview of Key Climatic and Mixed Hazards Mongolia Faces

Dzuds: These events normally occur when a severe summer drought is followed by an extreme winter. They have two primary causes: (i) meteorological conditions such as blizzards, heavy snow, extreme cold, and ice-bound pastures; and (ii) lack of available pasture due to droughts and overgrazing. The increase in the frequency of *dzuds* has dramatically heightened the risks of poverty for rural people, especially herders.[a]

Drought and water stress: Historically, drought in the spring and summer occurred about once every 5 years in the Gobi, and once every 10 years in other parts of the country. But since 1991, there has been some degree of drought in Mongolia every year.[b] The water resources of Mongolia—including groundwater—are under further stress due to the growing mining industry, increased herd sizes—especially cashmere goats—rapid urbanization that taxes limited water supply systems and sanitation services in the city, and an increase in temperature and evaporation rates caused by climate change.

Snowstorms and dust storms: Strong winds produce severe snowstorms in the fall and winter, and dust storms in the late winter and early spring. Windstorms remove the topsoil and make agriculture extremely difficult. The dust storms are particularly intense in the Gobi Desert region and are exacerbated during droughts. Since 2000, dust storms have been occurring earlier, with greater frequency, lasting longer, and carrying stronger winds and more dust. The winds also contribute to intense snowstorms and blizzards that can dump one meter of snow within a short time. These blizzards have been deadly in some years, especially in 2001 and 2008.[c]

Extreme cold and heat waves: These phenomena are common, and the patterns are changing. Since the 1940s the frequency of days of extreme high temperatures (i.e., maximum air temperature above 26°C) has increased on average by 16 to 25 days per year, and the frequency of days with extreme cold (minimum air temperature below –50°C) has decreased by 13 to 14 days per year.

Floods and landslides: The country is vulnerable to flooding. In the spring, snowmelt from the Mongolian Altai, Khovsgal, and Khangai mountain ranges often causes flooding in the rivers. Flash flooding and landslides can occur after a period of heavy rain, impacting livelihoods and claiming lives. In July 2018, heavy rainfalls caused flash floods in several parts of the country affecting almost 3,000 people. Flood risk in Ulaanbaatar City is being reduced by regulating floodplain settlement.[d]

Steppe and forest fires: Forests in Mongolia are found mostly in the permafrost area; they store carbon, protect soil from erosion, and regulate runoff, preserving water catchments. It is one of the most fire prone countries in Asia for both steppe and forest fires due to its low humidity and strong winds in the driest seasons. More than half of the country is susceptible to forest and grassland fires. Although up to 95% of these fires are caused by human activities, higher temperatures and recurrent dryness have facilitated conditions conducive to the occurrence and spread of fire.

Desertification, deforestation, and land degradation: This is due to a combination of overgrazing, poor land use practices such as the large-scale transformation of prairies into croplands, and excessive logging in the previous generation without effective reforestation, as well as wildfires. Climate change impacts are expected to exacerbate the rate of desertification and land degradation.

Air pollution in Ulaanbaatar and the provincial centers: The government defines air pollution as a climate change issue because of its close connection with emissions from coal-fired power stations near Ulaanbaatar (both GHGs and pollutants such as acid gases, mercury and other toxic metals) and increasing vehicle traffic. Coal remains the primary energy source. Demand is growing for both electricity and heating, and both are coal-based: Ulaanbaatar is heated with piped steam from the power stations, and in peri-urban areas briquettes made from coke powder are used in household stoves (since the burning of raw coal was banned). Air pollution in Ulaanbaatar from vehicle and coal emissions has at times required emergency mitigation response.

dzud = sudden freezing weather event, GHG = greenhouse gas.

[a] J. Neve. 2016. Climate Change and Savage Winters Fuel Urban Migration in Mongolia. International Organization for Migration (IOM). Press Release. 29 September.

[b] Center for Excellence in Disaster Management and Humanitarian Assistance. 2018. *Mongolia Disaster Management Reference Handbook*.

[c] J. Hays. 2019. *Weather and Climate of Mongolia*.

[d] Center for Excellence in Disaster Management and Humanitarian Assistance. 2018. *Mongolia Disaster Management Reference Handbook*.

Source: Asian Development Bank.

[24] Government of Mongolia, Ministry of Environment and Tourism. 2018. *Mongolia Third National Communication: Under the United Nations Framework Convention on Climate Change*. Ulaanbaatar.

These hazards directly impact lives and livelihoods and are felt differently by women and men. Yet, these differences are often not well understood due to the lack of sex-disaggregated data that is both quantitative and qualitative. This evidence does not yet exist in Mongolia, as in many countries in the Asian region. In absence of this data, a review of the socioeconomic profile of Mongolia can be used to understand the situation for women compared to men in the country and determine key gender-based inequalities and discrimination that exist and have the potential to impact women's capacity to build resilience.

Socioeconomic dimensions of gender, climate change, and disaster risk management. In addition to the direct impacts of climate change and disasters, many indirect effects are relevant in Mongolia. These include urban migration, changes like work, and new opportunities that can open up with investment in areas such as renewable energy and reforestation. Both direct and indirect impacts of climate change and hazards for women and men are determined by preexisting gender inequalities. A meta-analysis of reports on disasters in 141 countries found that gender differences in death rates were directly linked to women's economic and social rights; that in societies where women and men enjoyed equal rights there were no significant sex differences in the number of deaths.[25] The worst impacts on women from disasters and climate change—and the disadvantages that emerge in decision-making by societies on adaptation—happen because women are already structurally disadvantaged by entrenched gender inequality, direct and indirect discrimination, and social and economic disadvantage. Some key socioeconomic factors of Mongolian women are the levels of women in governance in 2021 (including Parliament, leadership, and decision-making positions), health status, education level, the types of economic sectors where women work, employment and working conditions, ownership of property and assets, and the overarching impact of GBV. These socioeconomic elements are discussed in the remainder of the profile for Mongolia.

Governance: In 1995 the United Nations Division of the Advancement of Women issued a report in which experts regarded 30% as being a critical minimum mass required for women as a group to exert a meaningful influence in legislative assemblies.[26] Data collected by IPU Parline in 2020 shows that Mongolia is well down the ranking and is 123rd out of 188 countries with a 17.33% representation of women in Parliament.[27] Women also remain underrepresented in civil service leadership roles, meaning they do not yet have a strong voice in the political and policy-making processes.[28] According to the 2020 Global Gender Gap Index of the World Economic Forum, the political empowerment of women was assessed as particularly low in Mongolia which was placed 120th out of the 152 countries listed.[29]

Health: Significant progress has been made in reducing maternal mortality and deaths among infants and children under five, which were key Millennium Development Goals.[30] However, such gains can be temporarily interrupted by climatic events coming on top of economic stresses. For example, there was a dramatic spike in maternal mortality rates in 2016 after an economic downturn had led to increased poverty as well as state budget cuts for contraceptives and other reproductive health supplies, and this was followed by a *dzud* that caused massive livestock loss and exacerbated health issues for rural women.[31]

Despite general progress on many health indicators, there are significant gender gaps in health between women and men. The average life expectancy for women in 2019 was 75.96 years, which was almost 10 years longer than men at 66.38 years.[32]

---

[25] E. Neumayer and T. Plumper. 2007. The Gendered Nature of Natural Disasters: The Impact of Catastrophic Events on the Gender Gap in Life Expectancy, 1981-2002. *Annals of the American Association of Geographers.* 97 (3). pp. 551–556.

[26] UN Division for the Advancement of Women. 2005. *Equal Participation of Women and Men in Decision-Making Processes, with Particular Emphasis on Political Participation and Leadership.* Report of the Expert Group Meeting. Ethiopia. 24–27 October.

[27] Inter-Parliamentary Union. 2020. *Percentage of Women in National Parliaments: 2020* (accessed in November 2021).

[28] World Economic Forum. 2021. *Data Explorer: Global Gender Gap Index 2020* (accessed in November 2021).

[29] World Economic Forum. 2019. The Global Gender Gap Report 2020. Geneva.

[30] Government of Mongolia, Center for Health Development. 2015. *Health Indicators 2015.* Ulaanbaatar.

[31] D. Tali. 2018. How Mongolia Revolutionized Reproductive Health for Nomadic Women. *The New Humanitarian.* 11 January.

[32] Government of Mongolia, NSO. 2021. *Mongolian Statistical Information Service.*

Human health impacts of climate change and hazards are less well documented. Migration to urban areas is partly triggered by climate change. Almost 50% of the population of Mongolia now lives in the capital city of Ulaanbaatar. The air pollution in Ulaanbaatar city is several times worse than the safe levels recommended by the World Health Organization throughout seven months of the year and has been attributed to the high levels of pulmonary diseases, asthma, and other respiratory diseases in the city, especially among children and the elderly.[33] Recent research also suggests a high impact of this air pollution on the health of pregnant women, fetus weights, and stillbirths.[34] This is a major health issue for both women and infants. A further concern is a disparity with access to water and sanitation between urban and rural areas. As of 2015, 94% of the urban population and only 50% of the rural population had access to safe drinking water. The situation is worse for sanitation: 66% of urban and 41% of rural populations use basic facilities (pit latrines), putting large parts of the population at increased risk of disease outbreaks.[35]

Education: Achieving gender parity in education has been one of the great achievements for Mongolia, and the "reverse gender gap" in education is often discussed. In 2019, enrollment in primary school for females was 96.7% and 97% for males[36] but at the higher levels of education, women are increasingly more educated than men, while the educational level of men is lower in rural areas.[37] The different educational attainment levels between women and men sometimes favor women, who are more likely than men to be employed in professional jobs. At the same time—unlike other developing countries—the educated are more affected by joblessness and the majority of these are younger and female.[38]

Economic sectors: The four leading economic sectors in Mongolia are (i) agriculture, forestry, fisheries, and hunting; (ii) wholesale and retail trade, car and motorcycle maintenance services; (iii) the processing industry; and (iv) the mining industry.[39] In 2018, the greatest economic sector for employment was in agriculture, forestry, fisheries, and hunting, with greater numbers of men (189,665) than women (146,318) (Figure 2).

The agriculture sector is unique in Mongolia and gender-specific historical circumstances are resulting from the nature of nomadic pastoralism which influences the gender relations of Mongolian women and men.[40] According to the National Statistics Office (NSO), in 2020 there were 181,000 herder households (19.9% of total households) and 242,000 households with livestock (26.6% of total households) in Mongolia.[41] While sex-disaggregated statistics on herders is not readily available, the Food and Light Industry Sector Strategy includes a valuable analysis of the wider sector and indicates that more young women are moving from rural areas into urban areas for education and employment opportunities. The food and light industry sector is becoming feminized with decreasing numbers of male employees, and occupational segregation is widening in the crop farming subsector due to the level of mechanization and the types of plantations.[42]

33   Government of Mongolia, NSO. 2019. *Air Pollution and Health Concerns in Ulaanbaatar*. Ulaanbaatar.
34   Government of Mongolia, Ministry of Labor and Social Protection and National Committee on Gender Equality. 2019. *Mongolia Gender Situational Analysis: Advances, Challenges and Lessons Learned since 2005*. Ulaanbaatar.
35   Government of Mongolia. 2019. Mongolia Voluntary Review Report 2019: Implementation of the Sustainable Development Goals. Ulaanbaatar.
36   Government of Mongolia, NSO. 2021. *Mongolian Statistical Information Service* (accessed in March 2021).
37   Government of Mongolia, NSO and International Labour Organization (ILO). 2019. *Accelerating the 2030 Sustainable Development Goals through Decent Work SDG Monitoring and Country Profile for Mongolia*. Ulaanbaatar; and Government of Mongolia, Ministry of Labor and Social Protection. 2019. *Mongolia Comprehensive National-Level Review: Responses to questionnaire on implementation of the Beijing Declaration and Platform for Action*. Ulaanbaatar.
38   Government of Mongolia, Ministry of Labor and Social Protection and National Committee on Gender Equality. 2019. *Mongolia Gender Situational Analysis: Advances, Challenges and Lessons Learned since 2005*. Ulaanbaatar.
39   Government of Mongolia, Ministry of Labor and Social Protection and National Committee on Gender Equality. 2019. *Mongolia Gender Situational Analysis: Advances, Challenges and Lessons Learned since 2005*. p. 24. Ulaanbaatar.
40   Government of Mongolia, Ministry of Food, Agriculture and Light Industry and National Committee on Gender Equality. 2018. *The Food, Agriculture and Light Industry Sector Gender-Responsive Policy (2018–2025)*.
41   Government of Mongolia, NSO. 2020. *Livestock Statistics 2020* (accessed June 2021).
42   Government of Mongolia, Ministry of Food, Agriculture and Light Industry and National Committee on Gender Equality. 2018. *The Food, Agriculture and Light Industry Sector Gender-Responsive Policy (2018–2025)*.

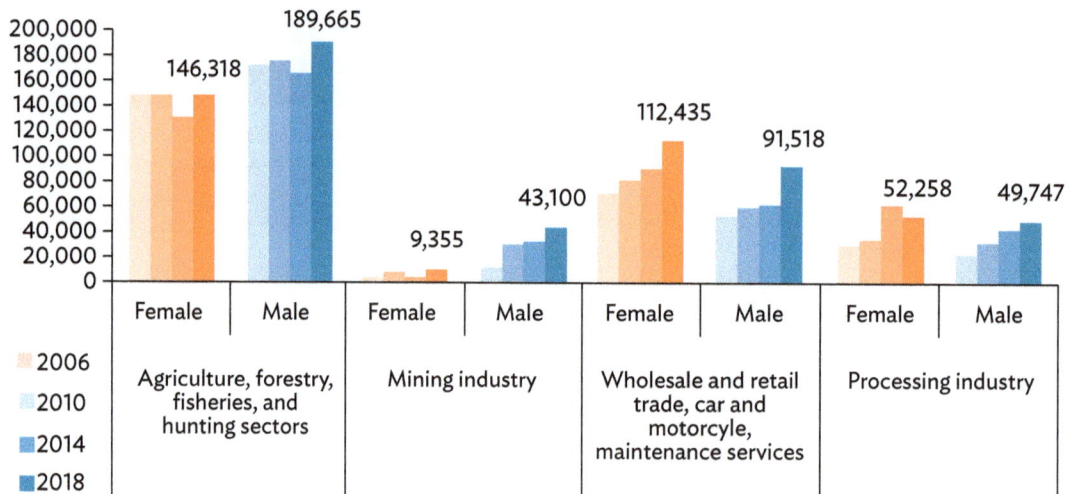

Figure 2: Number of Employees Engaged in Four Leading Economic Sectors in 2006–2018, by Gender

Source: Government of Mongolia, Ministry of Labor and Social Protection, and National Committee on Gender Equality. 2019. *Mongolia Gender Situational Analysis: Advances, Challenges and Lessons Learned since 2005*. Ulaanbaatar.

Employment and working conditions: Both women and men face different obstacles in employment because cultural norms and behaviors perpetuate stereotyped gender divisions of labor, which in turn affects decent work for women.[43] The obstacles for women include discrimination against them in employment and working conditions, including sexual harassment in the workplace and lower remuneration paid to working women compared to men, with a resultant gender wage gap. The labor force participation rates are much lower among women (53.4% in 2018) than among men (69.5% in 2018), and the disparity has been increasing.[44] This demonstrates that women have fewer opportunities than men to be engaged in productive employment.[45] The male–female informal employment ratio in Mongolia is high, and in 2016 almost 1:4 were in informal employment in nonagricultural activities with low levels of pay and conditions.[46] Overall, more men than women are in informal employment at a ratio of 8:5.[47]

There is also the issue of segmentation in the labor market between women and men:

(i)   **Horizontal segmentation.** Women are concentrated in the generally lower paid sectors of tourism and hospitality services, education, health and social support services, wholesale, and sales (formally and informally employed); men are concentrated in manufacturing, mining and other extractive industries, transport and energy (which are high-paid sectors)[48] as well as construction (formally and informally employed).[49]

---

[43]   Government of Mongolia, Ministry of Labor and Social Protection. 2019. *Mongolia Comprehensive National-Level Review: Responses to Questionnaire on Implementation of the Beijing Declaration and Platform for Action*. Ulaanbaatar.

[44]   Government of Mongolia, Ministry of Labor and Social Protection and National Committee on Gender Equality. 2019. *Mongolia Gender Situational Analysis: Advances, Challenges and Lessons Learned since 2005*. Ulaanbaatar.

[45]   Government of Mongolia, NSO and ILO. 2019. *Accelerating the 2030 Sustainable Development Goals through Decent Work SDG Monitoring and Country Profile for Mongolia*. Ulaanbaatar.

[46]   Government of Mongolia, NSO and ILO. 2019. *Accelerating the 2030 Sustainable Development Goals through Decent Work SDG Monitoring and Country Profile for Mongolia*. Ulaanbaatar.

[47]   A.D. Schmillen and N. Sandig. 2018. *Perceptions of Precariousness: A Qualitative Study of Constraints Underlying Gender Disparities in Mongolia's Labor Market*. Washington, DC. World Bank.

[48]   Green Climate Fund. 2019. *Country Programme Mongolia*.

[49]   Government of Mongolia, Ministry of Labor and Social Protection and National Committee on Gender Equality. 2019. *Mongolia Gender Situational Analysis: Advances, Challenges and Lessons Learned since 2005*. Ulaanbaatar.

(ii) **Vertical segmentation**. Men are clustered at the top of occupational hierarchies and women at the bottom, even in occupations that are female dominated. Generally, the share of women who are in managerial positions is around 36.7%, whereas women occupying professional positions is double that of men at 65.7%.[50]

(iii) While equal pay for the same job is applied in Mongolia (rather than equal remuneration for work of equal value, as discussed later in this report), the high degree of gender segmentation, and the fact that the jobs done predominantly by women are paid less on average, means there is still a gender wage gap of around 25%.

Workplace sexual harassment has serious impacts on women's health and well-being and their capacity to remain in secure long-term employment. In 2016, an online survey undertaken by the Mongolian Women's Fund revealed that 97.5% of victims of workplace sexual harassment were women, and 2.5% were men. The survey also showed that 97.5% of sexual harassment perpetrators were men and that 87.4% of them had higher education, and 69.1% were top executive managers.[51]

Land possession and housing ownership: A 2018 report found 60% of men and 33% of women in Mongolia owned their own homes, with 55% of men and 27% of women having officially registered their ownership rights.[52] In urban areas, 1.5 times more men than women have home ownership certificates and 3 times more men in rural areas.[53] A 2015 study among herder families established that 58.5% of household properties were registered under the names of men, 10.7% under the names of both spouses, and only 8.5% under the names of women.[54] A 2018 NSO study reported very low rates of documented (6% men versus 1% women) and reported (8% men versus 2% women) ownership of agriculture land, for both men and women.[55] In addition to land possession and use, herder families in Mongolia—which include herder women—are encountering serious challenges from natural hazards such as droughts and *dzuds* that affect land productivity.

Gender based violence: Several reports have highlighted the high incidence and prevalence of gender-based violence (GBV) in Mongolia.[56] According to the United Nations Population Fund (UNFPA), domestic violence is one of the most serious and common crimes in Mongolia, which is being committed regularly in violation of human rights.[57] The NSO 2017 national study revealed that around one in three women (35%) during the last year or in their current relationship, and more than half (59.7%) of all Mongolian women during their lifetime were subjected to physical, sexual, psychological, and economic violence. Ever-partnered women during last year or in a current relationship (SDG 5.2.1 indicator) experienced intimate partner violence at a rate of 12.7%, and 31.2% of them during their lifetime. Domestic violence acts were committed against women at a rate of 88.3% and against children at a rate of 64.6%. One-half of children and one-fourth of senior citizens are victims of domestic violence. The NSO report concluded that, unfortunately, the incidence of gravest violence-related crimes committed against women—such as domestic violence, human trafficking, and sexual harassment—had not dropped in the country despite new legislation.[58]

---

[50] Government of Mongolia, NSO and ILO. 2019. *Accelerating the 2030 Sustainable Development Goals through Decent Work SDG Monitoring and Country Profile for Mongolia*. Ulaanbaatar.

[51] Government of Mongolia, Ministry of Labor and Social Protection and National Committee on Gender Equality. 2019. *Mongolia Gender Situational Analysis: Advances, Challenges and Lessons Learned since 2005*. Ulaanbaatar.

[52] ADB. 2018. *Measuring Asset Ownership and Entrepreneurship from a Gender Perspective: Methodology and Results of Pilot Surveys in Georgia, Mongolia, and the Philippines*. Manila.

[53] Government of Mongolia, Ministry of Labor and Social Protection and National Committee on Gender Equality. 2019. *Mongolia Gender Situational Analysis: Advances, Challenges and Lessons Learned since 2005*. Ulaanbaatar.

[54] Swiss Agency for Development and Cooperation (SDC). 2015. *Gender analysis in pastoral livestock herding in Mongolia*. Ulaanbaatar.

[55] Government of Mongolia, National Statistics Office (NSO). 2018. *Measuring Asset Ownership and Entrepreneurship from a Gender Perspective: Pilot Study Report* (in original language). Ulaanbaatar.

[56] CEDAW. 2018. *Concluding Observations on the Combined Eighth and Ninth Periodic Reports of Mongolia*. New York; and Government of Mongolia, NSO and UNFPA. 2018. *Breaking the Silence for Equality 2017 National Study on Gender-Based Violence in Mongolia*; and Government of Mongolia, Ministry of Labor and Social Protection. 2019. *Mongolia Comprehensive National-Level Review: Responses to Questionnaire on Implementation of the Beijing Declaration and Platform for Action*. Ulaanbaatar.

[57] A. Esguerra and B. Oyun. 2016. Mongolian Parliament Approves Domestic Violence Law. *UNFPA News*. 26 May.

[58] Government of Mongolia, Ministry of Labor and Social Protection and National Committee on Gender Equality. 2019. *Mongolia Gender Situational Analysis: Advances, Challenges and Lessons Learned since 2005*. Ulaanbaatar.

The relevance of GBV—apart from the personal toll on women victims/survivors—is that it also has significant socioeconomic impacts on women generally and the community as a whole. It affects women's resilience to the impacts of climate change and disasters, which need to be strengthened and not further weakened. Prevention and mitigation of GBV also need to be included in disaster response planning for temporary shelters and ongoing access for affected communities—especially in rural areas—as services in Mongolia tend to be urban-centric.[59] Recent urban arrivals moving to escape rural disasters or impoverishment due to climate change may also need additional support services. International research indicates levels of violence are often exacerbated by disaster trauma, economic stress, and the pressures of mobility and changing family dynamics.[60]

This brief country profile presents the context of women's inequality and discrimination in Mongolia which poses serious threats to the socioeconomic situation of women and their ability to build resilience to climate and disaster risks. While this report recognizes the many successes in advancing gender equality in Mongolia, it also analyzes the gaps and needs that are not yet being addressed to build women's resilience. The next section of the report analyzes laws, policies, and institutions that are part of the framework to explore efforts by the Government of Mongolia to support women's resilience to climate change and disaster risk.

[59]   Z. Abdul Aziz and J. Moussa. 2016. *Due Diligence Framework: State Accountability for Eliminating Violence against Women*. Malaysia: Due Diligence Project.

[60]   International Federation of Red Cross and Red Crescent Societies. 2016. *Unseen, Unheard Gender-Based Violence in Disasters - Asia-Pacific Case Studies*. Kuala Lumpur.

2 Laws, Policies, and Institutions Supporting Women's Resilience to Climate Change and Disasters

2.1 National Structure for Gender Equality and Nondiscrimination

A good national structure to promote gender equality and prevent discrimination against women should have laws that guarantee the fundamental rights for women. Policies should further amplify legal provisions and implement legislative guarantees. These fundamental rights should preferably be expressed in a constitution, as this supreme law sets the platform for all laws. It emphasizes their importance and provides a sound basis for interpreting all other legislation. The essential concepts of equality and discrimination need to be visible in laws (Box 1).

The *National Good Practice Legislative Framework on Strengthening Women's Resilience to Climate Change and Disasters* presented in Section 1.3 (Figure 1) presents five key areas for analysis. Two are addressed in this section: (i) the Constitution of Mongolia, and (ii) national laws that prohibit gender discrimination and promote substantive equality.

Box 1: The Essential Concepts of Equality and Discrimination

The fundamental rights of equality and discrimination in relation to women include the concepts of ***formal equality*** (equal treatment of women and men); ***substantive equality*** (equality of outcome or results for women and men); promotion of equality (taking positive steps to achieve substantive equality); *prohibiting* **sex discrimination** both **direct discrimination** (laws, provisions or requirements, which expressly disadvantage women in comparison to men); and ***indirect discrimination*** (neutral laws, provisions or requirements, which have the effect of disadvantaging women in comparison to men); ***exceptions*** to discrimination (making allowances for biological difference such as pregnancy); ***exemptions*** from discrimination (where discriminating characteristics are inherent requirements for a particular job); and ***temporary special measures*** (taking positive measures to redress historical disadvantages to women and bring about substantive equality with men). These essential concepts of equality and discrimination need to be set out in legislation with a sufficient degree of specificity and detail, to enable them to be applied and enforced.

For further details and sources see Glossary.

2.1.1 Overview of Laws, Policies, and Institutions Related to Promoting Gender Equality and Nondiscrimination

The Constitution of Mongolia 1992 (Rev. 1999, 2001, and 2019) establishes the government and lawmaking structure. The national legislative body is the State Great Hural (State *Ikh Khural*), a single chamber Parliament with 76 members elected by the people for 4-year terms. The President is the head of state and commander-in-chief of the armed forces, directly elected by the people. The government (executive) is formed by the Prime Minister and ministers. The government is responsible for implementing legislation, initiating national, regional, and sector policies, and protecting human rights and freedoms, among other responsibilities. It is also empowered to make executive regulations that are consistent with the Constitution and legislation.

At the State Great Hural level, Mongolia has only 17.33% representation of women and it has been low for some years (e.g., 17.1% in 2016).[61] Quotas for determining the number of seats for equalizing the representation of women or men at political levels are authorized by the Law on the Promotion of Gender Equality (LPGE), however, no specific quota is set for the minimum number of seats to be represented in State Great Hural by women or men.[62] Quotas are one way to stress the importance of enshrining gender parity in the most important political body in the country and other countries have done this successfully, including Nepal[63] and Uganda.[64] Instead, the Law on Election 2016 requires that at least 20% of candidates nominated by a party must represent each gender (Article 126.2). This does not necessarily result in that percentage being elected. The international consensus is that quotas in legislation should be a minimum of 30% for one gender, which almost 30% of countries are achieving as of 2020.[65] The gender composition of Parliament is a factor that can affect the gender responsiveness of the law-making process and the content of laws, including those relating to environmental management, climate change, and disaster protection.

The two most important laws are the Law on Legislation 2015 and the LPGE, both of which have been gender analyzed, and the summary of findings presented in section 2.1.3. The Law on Legislation regulates the process of lawmaking; the purpose of the law is to improve the grounds and quality of legislation and to ensure public participation in the whole lawmaking process, as well as assessing the impact of laws to strengthen the rule of law. The LPGE establishes the legal basis for the creation of conditions to ensure gender equality in political, legal, economic, social, cultural, and family relations, and to regulate relations related to their implementation (Article 1). It is fundamental to the legal framework for gender equality and is linked to the Constitution (Article 2). Of all the laws—apart from the Constitution—the LPGE is pivotal to gender equality and nondiscrimination for women and men. The key policy document guiding the promotion of gender equality and prohibition of discrimination against women is the National Programme on Gender Equality 2017–2021 (NPGE). The goal of this policy is to support gender-responsive policy and planning processes required to reach the SDGs and to implement the LPGE.

The two key institutions for promoting gender equality and preventing discrimination are the National Committee on Gender Equality (NCGE) and the National Human Rights Commission (NHRC). The NCGE—which was set up in 1996 and moved under the Prime Minister Office in 2005 (named National Committee on Women's Issues)—is the national mechanism for implementing gender equality, and the essential functions of the NCGE are set out in a charter and establish gender councils and committees, as well as gender focal points within government ministries and provincial governments to oversee gender issues. The NCGE has 26 members with equal representation from state and civil society organizations. There are 31 gender committees in 21 *aimags* (provinces), in the capital city, and 9 districts and 13 sector-level gender councils at line ministries. This committee is important for addressing gender concerns to strengthen women's resilience to climate change and disasters. The functions that it performs include assisting ministries across the sectors to not only develop gender responsive policy but also to gender mainstream laws. In 2018, the NCGE Secretariat was restructured and given independent status working under the Prime Minister. Simultaneously, there was an increase in staff and budgetary operational expenses.[66]

---

61 Inter-Parliamentary Union. 2020. *Percentage of Women in National Parliaments: 2020* (accessed March 2021).

62 Government of Mongolia, National Committee on Gender Equality. *LPGE, National Program on Gender Equality and Its Action Plan*, Art. 7.7.2, on special measures.

63 The Constitution of Nepal 2015 requires at least one third of total members elected from each political party must be women. As of 1 March 2020, there were 32.73% of women in the lower house and 38.67% in the upper house, according to Inter-Parliamentary Union. 2020. *Percentage of Women in National Parliaments: 2020* (accessed in November 2021).

64 The Constitution of the Republic of Uganda 1995 (am 2005). Articles 78(1)(b),178 (2)(b), 180(2)(b) requires one third representation of women. As of 1 March 2021, there is 34.86% of women in Parliament, according to Inter-Parliamentary Union. 2020. *Percentage of Women in National Parliaments: 2020* (accessed in November 2021).

65 Inter-Parliamentary Union. 2020. *Percentage of Women in National Parliaments: 2020* (accessed in November 2021).

66 Government of Mongolia, National Committee on Gender Equality. 2019. *Mongolia Gender Situational Analysis: Advances. Challenges and Lessons Learned since 2005.* Ulaanbaatar.

The NHRC, which was set up in 2001, has a very broad mandate under the National Human Rights Commission of Mongolia Law 2000 (NHRC Law).[67] It is mandated to promote and protect human rights and to monitor the implementation of the provisions of human rights and freedoms provided in the Constitution of Mongolia, laws, and international treaties of Mongolia (Article 3.1). This includes the resolution of complaints about violations of the provisions of the LPGE (Article 23). The commission originally comprised three commissioners (which became five in 2020, with discussion to include one more member) and staff. The complaints mechanism enables "eligible complainants" (including citizens, either individually or in a group) to complain of violations of human rights by a public authority or a business. Examples of complaints that are within the jurisdiction of the NHRC—as reported to Parliament in its two-yearly status report—relate to complaints of domestic violence, sex discrimination, and sexual harassment in employment, as defined in the LGPE. Despite the simplicity of the complaint mechanism, the NHRC received only 22 complaints on gender-based discrimination in 2015–2016 and 240 complaints related to labor rights during 2008–2017.[68] Only 21 complaints during 2015–2019 were related to sexual harassment at the workplace (most of which were related to officials and decision-makers of public organizations).[69]

2.1.2 The Constitution of Mongolia

The Constitution strongly affirms the fundamental principles of the state to secure "democracy, justice, freedom, equality, national unity and the rule of law" (Article 1). It also imports—into domestic law—the principles of international law and the treaties to which Mongolia has acceded, meaning that the CEDAW Convention and other human rights conventions are part of Mongolian law. This is further strengthened by conferring an individual the right to appeal to the court to enforce these constitutional rights, including any rights under a treaty that has been violated. As many laws of Mongolia refer to the Constitution and require the law to be consistent with its contents, the principles of international law and treaties are therefore brought into that law.

There are seven provisions of the Constitution particularly important to supporting women's equality, empowerment, and resilience to climate and disaster risk. The Constitution

(i)   requires equality before the law and the courts (Article 14 [1]);

(ii)   prohibits discrimination on a range of grounds, including sex (Article 14 [2]);

(iii)   confers a right to a healthy and safe environment, and to be protected against environmental pollution and ecological imbalance (Article 16 [2]);

(iv)   confers a right to material and financial assistance in childbirth and childcare (Article 16 [5]);

(v)   establishes that men and women enjoy equal rights in political, economic, social, and cultural fields as well as in marriage (Article 16 [11]);

(vi)   requires that the State "protects the interests of the family, motherhood, and the child" (Article 16 [11]); and

(vii)   provides that every citizen has a sacred duty to work, protect their health, bring up and educate their children, and protect nature and the environment (Article 17 [2]).

In the context of climate change, Articles 16 (2) and 17 (2) are good legal practice examples of a mutual right to a healthy and safe environment and an obligation to protect nature and the environment. Although some of the fundamental principles of equality and nondiscrimination are not set out in the Constitution, they are set out comprehensively in the LPGE, which is gender analyzed in section 2.1.3.

---

67   There is now a new 2020 Law on National Human Rights Commission of Mongolia.

68   Government of Mongolia, Ministry of Labor and Social Protection. 2019. *Mongolia Comprehensive National-Level Review: Responses to Questionnaire in Implementation of the Beijing Declaration and Platform for Action.* Ulaanbaatar.

69   Government of Mongolia, Ministry of Labor and Social Protection and National Committee on Gender Equality. 2019. *Mongolia Gender Situational Analysis: Advances, Challenges and Lessons Learned since 2005.* Ulaanbaatar.

2.1.3   Gender Analysis Summary of Key Laws and Policies on Gender Equality and Nondiscrimination

A gender analysis was conducted of the key laws and policies to promote gender equality and prevent discrimination (Table 2). The color coded system is used to categorize the laws and policies and demonstrates the state of gender mainstreaming as of 2021.

Table 2: Summary of the Gender Equality and Nondiscrimination Framework

Law/Policy	Summary of Gender References
Law on Promotion of Gender Equality 2011 (LPGE)	There are definitions of essential concepts of equality and discrimination in alignment with international standards (CEDAW) and examples of the gender responsive approach are the guarantee of equal rights in the civil service (Article 10) and under special measures (Article 7).
Law on Legislation 2015	There is one mention of "equality" in the Constitution of Mongolia in Article 1. However, there were no other mention of gender issues or gender responsive approaches in the lawmaking process.
National Programme on Gender Equality 2017–2021 (NPGE)	The six objectives cover areas such as women's equal benefit from development gains, gender responsive policy, planning and budgeting processes, changing stereotypes and preventing gender-based violence, and encouraging women's participation in politics and decision making.

CEDAW = Convention on the Elimination of All Forms of Discrimination Against Women.
Note: Color coding: gender responsive (green), gender sensitive (yellow), not yet gender mainstreamed (orange).
Source: Asian Development Bank.

The LPGE is gender responsive. It is a good practice example expressing guarantees of the essential concepts of equality and discrimination and includes "promotion" of gender equality, which overall accords with CEDAW definitions and implementation requirements. It includes definitions of gender, gender equality, gender stereotypes, discrimination (direct and indirect), sexual harassment, gender-based violence, and refers to special measures and gender quotas. Conversely, the Law on Legislation is categorized as not yet gender mainstreamed as there is no reference to roles and responsibilities of women or men, no reference to gender, and nothing to indicate that a gender sensitive or responsive approach is required in the lawmaking process. Article 4 of the Law on Legislation has a limited reference to Article 1 paragraph 2 of the Constitution on "equality" but there are no provisions in it that incorporate important principles and approaches provided for in relevant articles of the LPGE.

The NPGE Policy and its action plan are also categorized as gender responsive. The policy expresses six program objectives to achieve the goal and each of these is underpinned by implementation activities. There is also an associated Action Plan on the Implementation of the NPGE which proposes 59 activities.

Two reports in 2019 describe the spread of achievements, challenges, and setbacks in progress for Mongolia towards gender equality and the empowerment of women which indicate that Mongolia has already made significant gains for gender equality.[70] In particular, the LPGE is considered global best practice. It has generated rapid development of gender-responsive strategies in the following sectors: environment (which is discussed later in this report);[71] finance;[72] justice and internal affairs;[73] education, culture, science, and sports;[74] population, labor, and

---

[70]   Government of Mongolia, Ministry of Labor and Social Protection and National Committee on Gender Equality. 2019. *Mongolia Gender Situational Analysis: Advances, Challenges and Lessons Learned since 2005*; and Ministry of Labor and Social Protection. 2019. *Mongolia Comprehensive National-Level Review: Responses to questionnaire on implementation of the Beijing Declaration and Platform for Action*. Ulaanbaatar.

[71]   Government of Mongolia, Ministry of Environment and Tourism. 2014. *Environmental Sector Gender Strategy 2014–2030*. Ulaanbaatar.

[72]   Government of Mongolia, Ministry of Finance. 2018. *Gender Strategy for Organizations and Agencies under the Authority of the Minister of Finance of Mongolia (2016–2024)*. Ulaanbaatar.

[73]   Government of Mongolia, Ministry of Justice and Home Affairs. 2018. *The Gender-Responsive Integrated Policy of Law Enforcement Organizations Under the Authority of the Minister of Justice and Home Affairs (2018–2021)*. Ulaanbaatar.

[74]   Government of Mongolia, Ministry of Education, Culture, Science and Sports. 2018. *The Education, Culture, Science and Sports Sector Gender-Responsive Policy (2017–2024)*. Ulaanbaatar.

social protection;[75] construction and urban development;[76] food, agriculture, and light industry;[77] geology, mining, petroleum, and heavy industry.[78] Three ministries—the Ministry of Mining and Heavy Industry, the Ministry of Defense, and the Ministry of Foreign Affairs—conducted participatory gender assessments with the involvement of sector employees and independently developed sector gender policies in 2020. The gender responsive sector strategies under the LPGE are still being developed or are in the early stages of implementation. As of 2021, a gender responsive policy had not been developed for emergency management or energy.

The comprehensive national structure on gender equality in Mongolia is at a very high government level and demonstrates significant political commitment to achieve gender equality. The LPGE and NPGE provide a solid foundation to promote gender responsive sector laws and policies.

2.2 Gender and Disaster Risk Management

Disasters can affect men and women differently depending on gender roles in the type of work and family caring responsibilities. With Mongolian women earning less than men on average and having less access to land and housing, they may also suffer greater relative economic losses and longer recovery times if they lose their homes or possessions. This can also increase their unpaid workload of home and caring duties following disasters. The situation of herder families is also unique to Mongolia. Weather-related hazards impact greatly on their livelihoods.[79] Although they work as family economic units it is important to look at gender roles within family structures to understand whether special measures are needed to address gender-based vulnerabilities or the needs of women or men in disasters. This would be distinct but in addition to understanding climate change and disaster risks for urban men and women. Gender profiles—which examine gender roles and responsibilities and socioeconomic status in normal times—can play important role in disaster risk management and should feed into law and policy related decision making.

2.2.1 Overview of Key Laws, Policies, and Institutions Related to the Disaster Risk Management System

The Mongolia system for DRM is based around the Law on Disaster Protection 2003 (Rev. 2017), on constitutional emergency powers, and civil defense institutions at national and subnational levels established as part of government administration.[80] The national State Emergency Commission is the high-level policy and decision-making body during emergencies, while the National Emergency Management Agency (NEMA) is the national coordinator and operational responder which employs disaster protection service staff and develops DRM policies and plans.[81] NEMA is a paramilitary organization—using military ranks and organizational style—and some staff training is in common with the military. The Law on the Defense of Mongolia also allows for use of the active military for humanitarian relief during disasters.[82]

---

[75]   Government of Mongolia, Ministry of Population, Labor and Social Protection. 2018. *The Population, Labor and Social Protection Sector Gender-Responsive Policy (2018–2024)*. Ulaanbaatar.

[76]   Government of Mongolia, Ministry of Construction and Urban Development. 2018. *The Construction and Urban Development Sector Gender-Responsive Policy (2018–2025)*. Ulaanbaatar.

[77]   Government of Mongolia, Ministry of Food, Agriculture and Light Industry. 2018. *The Food, Agriculture and Light Industry Sector Gender-Responsive Policy (2018–2025)*. Ulaanbaatar.

[78]   Government of Mongolia, Ministry of Mining. 2019. *The Geology, Mining, Petroleum and Heavy Industry Sector Gender Responsive Policy (2019–2026)*. Ulaanbaatar.

[79]   International Federation of Red Cross and Red Crescent Societies. 2016. *Mongolia extreme weather condition emergency appeal operations update n° 1.*

[80]   Government of Mongolia. n.d. *Law on Disaster Protection 2003* (Rev. 2017)[original language].

[81]   Center for Excellence in Disaster Management and Humanitarian Assistance. 2018. *Mongolia Disaster Management Reference Handbook.* pp. 22–24.

[82]   Parliament of Mongolia, Standing Committee on Security and Foreign Policy, the Geneva Centre for the Democratic Control of Armed Forces, and the Ulaanbaatar Center for Policy Studies. 2017. *Security Sector Governance in Mongolia: Almanac 2017.* pp. 51, 55, 86. Ulaanbaatar.

The relevant DRM policy is the National Programme of Community Participation Disaster Risk Reduction (2015–2025) which has the goal to "Reduce disaster risks through involvement of communities and individuals in activities of disaster prevention, enhancement of their knowledge and skills due to training and education, promotion and communication, in the creation of safe living culture and strengthening resilience to climate change."[83] The program envisages a high level of community engagement and capacity building on disaster and climate risk reduction. It is managed and organized by NEMA and the subnational and local levels of the DRM system.

The system for disaster protection and the national approach to climate change have not been integrated in Mongolia as of 2021. The DRM system does not have formalized links with the institutional frameworks for managing climate change risk within the Ministry for the Environment and Tourism (MET).[84]

2.2.2 Gender Analysis Summary of Key Disaster Risk Management Laws and Policies

A gender analysis was conducted of the laws and policies relevant to DRM (Table 3). The color coded system is used to categorize the laws and policies and demonstrates the state of gender mainstreaming as of 2021.

Table 3: Summary of Gender Inclusion in Disaster Risk Management

Law/Policy	Summary of Gender References
Law on Disaster Protection (LDP) 2003, revised 2017	Equality and nondiscrimination provisions of the Constitution, and other national laws and international treaties, are included by Article 2 as is the common system in Mongolia. This Article enables the provisions in the Constitution on equality and nondiscrimination to be utilized in the interpretation and application of the LDP to benefit women yet there is no other mention of women or gender issues in the LDP.
National Programme of Community Participatory Disaster Risk Reduction (2015–2025)	The policy describes stakeholders as citizens, entities and organizations, local self-governance institutions, and governmental administrative and local administrative institutions. The program conceptualization of stakeholders does not allow for consideration of cross-cutting social categorization such as gender. There is no mention or link to other legislation or policies that promote gender equality.

Note: Color coding: gender responsive (green), gender sensitive (yellow), not yet gender mainstreamed (orange).
Source: Asian Development Bank.

As of 2021, neither of the two key instruments for DRM acknowledge the gender dimensions of disaster risk in Mongolia. Throughout most of the 52 Articles of the LDP, reference is made to the people concerned as citizens, employees, employers, people, owners of property, and not to men, or women, or gender. There are two very minor references to women and/or gender:

(i)   In Article 24 on Disaster Protection Manpower, in which Article 24.2 states that "Specialised units shall be formed by Mongolian citizens with the ability to work, males of 18–60 years of age and females of 18–55" (with some exclusions); and

(ii)   In Article 40.4, international humanitarian assistance providers are prohibited from discrimination based on nationality, ethnicity, age, gender, social origin, status, religion, or political opinion.

These minor mentions of males and/or females and gender highlight the absence of any reference to these categories in any other aspect of the priorities or organizational structures set up under the legislation. For example, chapters five and six of the law set out the management and organizational structures and their powers, including the roles

---

[83]   Government of Mongolia. 2015. *Approval of a National Programme*. Unofficial translation. p. 4. Ulaanbaatar.

[84]   Government of Mongolia, Ministry of Environment and Tourism. 2018. *Mongolia Third National Communication: Under the United Nations Framework Convention on Climate Change*. Ulaanbaatar.

of the Disaster Risk Reduction National Council, equivalent local councils, the State Emergency Commission, the National Emergency Management Agency, and central and local government administrations. These bodies are not established by the law, so the law itself does not provide insight into membership and criteria, nor methods of appointment to them. There is no requirement that they involve women or anyone with expertise in gender analysis.

Overall, the LDP does not address gender as an issue or priority in disaster protection and assumes that men and women have the same types of needs and experience disasters in much the same way; it effectively assumes that there are no gender differences to consider. Thus, the LDP neither provides for gender analysis of disaster risk or impacts nor provides gender balance in representation in institutions and decision-making roles. Similarly, the National Programme of Community Participation Disaster Risk Reduction also fails to mention the gender differences in community management of disaster risk. Rather, it describes the stakeholders as citizens, entities and organizations, local self-governance institutions, and governmental and local administrative institutions, assuming that women and men experience disaster risk in the same way.

The collection and analysis of sex-disaggregated data are acknowledged as critical to understanding disaster risk and provide evidence on the gendered dimension of disaster risk. While disaster impact data collection is well advanced in Mongolia,[85] especially since 2000,[86] data are disaggregated by hazard event, disaster type (such as floods or storms), geographical location, age (e.g., adult and children), and year. Data is not yet collected on (dis) abilities of people, income, or age disaggregation. Although data on the sex of individuals affected by disasters has reportedly been collected, sex-disaggregated data has not been systematically analyzed, although NEMA has begun to do so.[87] The important next step will be the analysis of such disaggregated data and its application to ensure gender-responsive decision making.

2.3 Gender, Climate Change, and Environmental Management

The impacts of climate change on the environment in Mongolia give added importance to environmental regulation beyond traditional concepts of protecting the environment and ecosystems. The law and policy framework must increasingly deal with rising temperatures, greater weather extremes, long term changes in plant and animal life, groundwater and rainfall, and the impacts of these on ecosystems. Along with human activity, such factors contribute to desertification and land degradation and require adaptations in land use and changes to traditional rural livelihoods. This leads to greater competition for resources, and pressure to put shorter-term economic needs ahead of sustainable development. Well-managed change can provide opportunities for positive social change including improved gender equality in access to environmental resources.

Data on the different impacts of climate change and environmental degradation on women and men are lacking in Mongolia, similar to the data gaps in DRM. However, recent studies and small-scale assessments are being conducted which point to how gender roles and responsibilities result in differential impacts and where laws and policies are needed to ensure gender equality in the pursuit of climate action and environmental management (Box 2).

---

[85]   Data are collected by the Local Emergency Management Departments and the Disaster Research Institute under the National Emergency Management Agency (NEMA), with inputs from the local governmental administration offices.

[86]   Center for Excellence in Disaster Management and Humanitarian Assistance. 2018. *Mongolia Disaster Management Reference Handbook.*

[87]   Aa advised by NEMA during project workshop in November 2019.

> ### Box 2: Gender Roles and Responsibilities in Forestry in Mongolia
>
> According to a 2018 gender assessment of forestry in Mongolia, men and women play quite different roles, which stakeholders attribute to men and women's different physical strengths and duties in the household. The study reported that "men participate more in physical or guarding works, and women's participation is more in the reproductive activities such as taking care of seedlings, tree planting, and forest restoration activities..." Stakeholders, especially men, "tend to regard forestry business in Mongolia as a male-dominant sector," and there is an emphasis on protecting women against illegal logging, fires, and dangerous work. Although there is a lack of sex-disaggregated data on employment in forest industries, survey perceptions were that men are concentrated in wood-processing companies, doing timber harvesting, sawmilling and small-scale furniture and joinery, while women are more likely to be in non-timber forest user groups (FUGs), although younger women and men are not significantly engaged in FUGs. The study also indicated that gender inequality in forestry is intersectional, linked to increasing rural poverty and emerging educational disadvantage in rural areas, as well as lower representation of women in decision-making positions across the public and private sectors.
>
> Source: GIZ Mongolia, Independent Research Institute of Mongolia, Ministry of Environment and Tourism. 2018. *Analysis of the Gender Equality Situation in Environmental Sector (in the Case of Forestry Sector)* Final Report. Chicago.

2.3.1 Overview of Laws, Policies, and Institutions Related to Climate Change and Environmental Management

The overarching law on human welfare and the environment is the Constitution of Mongolia, which guarantees citizens "the right to a healthy and safe environment, and to be protected against environmental pollution and ecological imbalance."[88] The main sector-wide laws on the environment and natural resources that relate to climate change are the Law on Environmental Protection (LEP) and the Law on Environmental Impact Assessments (EIA Law). The LEP stated purpose is to "regulate relations between the State, citizens, business entities and organizations in order to guarantee the human right to live in a healthy and safe environment, an ecologically balanced social and economic development, the protection of the environment for present and future generations, the proper use of natural resources and the restoration of available resources" (Article 1). The EIA Law specifically seeks to integrate environmental assessments with the process of developing policies and programs locally and centrally, including the context of climate change (Article 1, 3.1).[89]

Specific aspects of environmental laws are then regulated by the Law on Forests, the Law on Water, the Law on Land, and the Law for Soil Protection and Prevention of Desertification, among others. There is no separate law on climate change, but the 2012 Law on Air includes provisions on ozone layer protection, monitoring of GHG emissions, and preparation of a GHG inventory. Other climate change adaptation and mitigation laws analyzed in this report are the Law on Disaster Protection (previously discussed in 2.2), and energy laws (discussed in 2.4).

On the policy side, the Government of Mongolia has adopted a range of national and sector policies and strategies that address climate change adaptation and mitigation directly in the context of sustainable development. The principal policies are (i) the National Action Plan on Climate Change (2011–2021) and the process to update it; (ii) the National Green Development Policy (2014–2030); (iii) the updated Nationally Determined Contribution (NDC) under the UNFCCC as part of the commitments to the Paris Agreement; (iv) the Third National Communication of Mongolia under the UNFCCC; and (v) the Mongolia Sustainable Development Vision 2030 and Vision 2050.

---

[88]   Parliament of Mongolia. 1992. *Constitution of Mongolia 1992* (Rev. 2019), Art. 16(2). Ulaanbaatar.
[89]   Parliament of Mongolia. n.d. *Law on Environmental Impact Assessments 1998* (Rev. 2011). Ulaanbaatar.

The Ministry of Environment and Tourism (MET) of Mongolia is the government body responsible for both environmental protection and the national coordination of action on climate change.[90] Following a major government review of the environmental laws, Mongolia made a suite of reforms and rationalizations in 2012.[91]

2.3.2 Gender Analysis Summary of Key Climate and Environmental Laws and Policies

A gender analysis was conducted of the select laws and policies relevant to climate change and environmental protection (Table 4). The color coded system is used to categorize the laws and policies and demonstrates the state of gender mainstreaming as of 2021.

Table 4: Summary of Gender Inclusion in Climate and Environmental Laws and Policies

Law/Policy	Summary of Gender References
Law on Environmental Protection (LEP) 1995 (Rev. 2008);	Gender equality and nondiscrimination are part of the legal framework because the law incorporates the Constitution and other national laws and international treaties (Article 2). But the law does not directly address gender or the separate concerns of men and women. As of 2021, no provision in the law requires the inclusions of gender equality outcomes, gender-sensitive processes, or gender mainstreaming.
Law on Environmental Impact Assessments (EIA Law) 1998 (Rev. 2011)	Gender equality and nondiscrimination are part of the legal framework because the law incorporates the Constitution and other national laws and international treaties (Article 2). But the law does not directly address gender or the separate concerns of men and women. As of 2021, no provision in the law requiring gender assessment, gender-sensitive processes, or gender mainstreaming.
Law on Forests 1995 (Rev. 2013)	The Law on Forests brings gender equality and nondiscrimination into its regulatory framework by incorporating the Constitution and other national laws and international treaties (Article 2). But it does not give any guidance on how to implement gender-inclusion in the forest sector.
Law on Water 2004 (Rev. 2011)	The Law on Water brings gender equality and nondiscrimination into its regulatory framework by incorporating the Constitution and other national laws and international treaties in the same manner as the other environmental laws. But it does not give any guidance on how to implement gender-inclusion in water management.
Law on Land 2002 (Rev. 2018)	The Law on Land brings gender equality and nondiscrimination into its regulatory framework by incorporating the Constitution and other national laws and international treaties in the same manner as the other environmental laws. But it does not give any guidance on how to implement gender-inclusion in land management.
National Action Programme on Climate Change (NAPCC) 2011	This policy includes the concept of gender equality in its implementation principles (section 2.4), although no specific policy action on gender equality for women. It mentions the need to promote the participation of women in international and regional activities and forums, although again this is not specific (section 3.5.8).
National Green Development Policy (NGDP) 2014	The NGDP does not consider women's equality or gender issues as a specific objective, but it does include, Under Strategic objective 4 on reducing poverty and promoting green jobs, and a proposal to offer salaries for women taking care of children.
Nationally Determined Contribution (Updated, 2020)	The document notes that vulnerable 'social groups' need to be identified and the need to ensure equality for the vulnerable social groups in providing social safeguards and prevention measures. There is no mention of gender, gender equality, or women and men.

continued on next page

---

[90] A Climate Change Committee or Commission is mentioned in several international reports, but this is no longer in place and structures within the Ministry relating to climate change were not yet settled as of 2021.

[91] United Nations Economic Commission for Europe. 2018. *Environmental Performance Review of Mongolia.*

Table *continued*

Law/Policy	Summary of Gender References
Sustainable Development Vision 2030	The document mentions gender equality in the context of the goal for sustainable social development and its subsection on ensuing equality through sustainable growth. It does not have any specific gender components, actions, or objectives related to women.
Third National Communication (Submitted to UNFCCC 2018)	Despite being developed during the implementation of the gender sector strategy, the only mention of women and/or gender is in reporting different life expectancies. There is no discussion of gender differences in climate change impacts or policy responses.
Environmental Sector Gender Strategy 2014–2030	The three strategic goals include (i) build capacities to carry out gender analysis and gender responsive planning, (ii) gender sensitization of the environmental sector and management practices, and (iii) expand participation of women and men in different social groups and local communities in green development processes and open up broader avenues for their equal access to benefits.

UNFCCC = United Nations Framework Convention on Climate Change.
Note: Color coding: gender responsive (green), gender sensitive (yellow), not yet gender mainstreamed (orange).
Source: Asian Development Bank.

Three key laws analyzed in depth (LEP, EIA Law, and the Law on Forests) are examples of the style of sector law used in Mongolia that provides for formal equality but does not include mandates or mechanisms for special measures to achieve substantive gender equality. Each law treats the scope of regulation as either neutral technical issues or social issues that are presumed to impact equally on all people. They formally incorporate the equality and nondiscrimination provisions of the Constitution, but they do not expressly incorporate the LPGE and do not provide any mechanisms for gender analysis of policies and plans, gender-sensitive processes or mechanisms for public, community, and civil society participation, or gender mainstreaming in implementation.

In terms of public participation in environmental protection, several laws include citizen rights to object, to be heard, and to be compensated for damage, as well as civil society action through nongovernment organizations recognized under the LEP as organizations formed to protect the environment (Article 4). However, no laws mention methodologies for public participation and how to ensure gender inclusive approaches through the inclusion of women-focused organizations. One missed opportunity to mandate gender-inclusive processes is in the EIA Law. While the regulatory scope of the law is broad, the project and local area assessments occur in specific environments with specific populations. In these cases, it would be possible to examine more closely, any differential impacts on men and women in the local economy and residential community. Existing legal mechanisms for public and community consultations during EIAs could be adapted by requiring assessments to be gender-sensitive and setting out a methodology to do this. There is already the capacity for ministerial regulations on public and community consultations which could be used to require gender inclusive processes.

The National Action Programme on Climate Change (NAPCC)—the main climate change policy driving government programs since 2011—aims to help Mongolia create the capacity to adapt to climate change and establish green economic growth and development. Its goals include environmental sustainability, socioeconomic development adapted to climate change, reduction of GHG emissions, vulnerabilities, and risks.[92] The NAPCC includes the concept of gender equality in its implementation principles (section 2.4), which is a good practice example, although it does not include specific policy actions on gender equality for women. It also mentions the need to promote the participation of women in international and regional activities and forums, although again this is not specific (section 3.5.8).

---

[92] Parliament of Mongolia. 2011. *National Action Programme on Climate Change.* Ulaanbaatar.

Other policies—such as the Sustainable Development Vision 2030—also mention ensuring equality—in this case through sustainable growth—and the NGDP refers to reducing poverty and the role of unpaid labor by women. No other policy documents mention essential concepts of equality and nondiscrimination. The other policies reviewed do not include any objectives related to gender roles of men and women or specific gender-based vulnerabilities to climate change or environmental degradation. Both the Third National Communication and the NDC update were also missed opportunities to integrate the LPGE and associated gender commitments, particularly given the increasing global push to integrate gender and social inclusion into UNFCCC processes.

In terms of sex-disaggregated data on climate change impacts, there are insufficient approaches and commitments to collect this data as of 2021. Data on climate change impacts (such as climate hazards) are gathered systematically by the Ministry for the Environment and Tourism as the national focal point under the international climate change treaties. Key data is summarized in Mongolia's 2018 Third National Communication under the UNFCCC and in the 2020 NDC Update Submission under the Paris Agreement. There is no discussion of gender differences in climate change impacts or policy responses in either of these documents.

The one piece of environmental policy that actively promotes gender equality is the Environmental Sector Gender Strategy. This is the first sector strategy adopted by the government to implement the LPGE, and this gender responsive strategy has three strategic goals. The first two are primarily concerned with process: setting up the framework, and capacity to act on gender equality in the sector to (i) increase understanding of gender mainstreaming; (ii) develop gender-sensitive analytical and planning tools; (iii) address management practices to make planning more gender-sensitive; (iv) facilitate participation at all levels, especially for women; and (v) improve coherence and gender-responsiveness of sector and local planning. The third strategy then addresses how to promote gender equality within development planning—especially in green development processes in Mongolia—through increased community participation and equal access to benefits.[93]

An analysis of the Environmental Sector Gender Strategy shows that although it is commendably ambitious in what it hopes to achieve, it often does not provide detailed guidance on achievable and concrete activities towards its objectives. The nine-page Annex I to the strategy sets out the activities to be undertaken in each phase of implementation; there are 24 activities and outputs listed for Phase 1—the first 2 years—and slightly more for each of the subsequent phases. These activities are large in number, and most of them are very substantial pieces of work in their own right that would require both staff time and significant commitment of resources to achieve in the time frames given, and most are not broken down into specific practical milestones. It is therefore understandable that it has faced implementation challenges.[94] The independent review of Phase 1 found that only a small proportion of the activities had been achieved, especially as the budget and other resources committed to it were unspecified and very low. There was also not a clear decision-making structure to implement the strategy within the sector.[95]

Overall, gender considerations have not been a significant part of environmental law and policy in Mongolia, but importantly, the very first sector gender strategy demonstrates an initial commitment and a foundation on which to build. It is understood that implementation of the gender strategy has now been assessed but the report was not available at the time of writing in 2021.

93   Government of Mongolia, Ministry of Environment and Tourism. 2014. *Environmental Sector Gender Strategy 2014–2030*. Ulaanbaatar.
94   Government of Mongolia, Ministry of Labor and Social Protection and National Committee on Gender Equality. 2019. *Mongolia Gender Situational Analysis: Advances, Challenges and Lessons Learned since 2005*. Ulaanbaatar.
95   Deutsche Gesellschaft für Internationale Zusammenarbeit (GIZ) Mongolia, Independent Research Institute of Mongolia, Government of Mongolia Ministry of Environment and Tourism. 2018. *Assessment of the Environmental Sector Gender Strategy Phase 1 (2014–2016)*.

2.4 Gender and the Energy Sector

There is a direct link between climate change and the energy sector, particularly in Mongolia where the major source of energy is coal. Both mining and the use of coal are associated with grave environmental and health challenges as well as contributing to global warming. However, economic pressure to continue relying on coal comes from the fact that energy needs in Mongolia are increasing rapidly and the country has such vast reserves of it. This sector was chosen for particular analysis in this report due to the increasing demands for energy in Mongolia, the specific gender issues related to energy access and use, as well as the fact that laws and policies in Mongolia are evolving as part of their commitments under the Paris Agreement.

2.4.1 Overview of the Energy Sector

The energy sector is very complex and only a snapshot of some important features can be described here. Coal-fired power stations in Mongolia are directly linked to an established city heating system in Ulaanbaatar, as they provide steam for the system of piped hot water heating throughout the city; thus, a distinction is made between energy production for heating and electricity. The heating season is unusually long at 8 months and energy demand for heating is more than double that for electricity. Since coal is a dominant source for the production of both electricity and heat generation, combined heat and power (CHP) has been regarded as the most suitable, efficient, and economical technology choice to provide both electricity and heat.[96]

Energy demand now needs to accommodate increasing population influx and economic concentration which pushes electricity and heat load demand growth further. Heat load demand in Ulaanbaatar grew by 35% during 2006–2016 and is projected to grow even higher by 2030, risking energy security for many across the country. [97] However, facilities for providing heating and electricity are energy inefficient and vulnerable because they are old and outdated.[98] They are in urgent need of rehabilitation and upgrade, and they rely very significantly on fossil fuels.

Ger (traditional tent dwelling) areas surrounding Ulaanbaatar now account for 60% of city residents and with increasing urbanization, these areas are placing a strain on already stretched energy demands. Gers are not part of the city heating system, although the electricity grid is being constantly extended to these new settlements as they are formalized. Residents in these areas use coal-based household stoves and often additional small, inefficient, electric hotplates for cooking.[99] Raw coal was banned for health reasons effective February 2019, and instead, household stoves use government-subsidized coke briquettes and wood to fire them up. These ger areas have also had the benefit of the 175,000 clean stoves initiative financed by the World Bank and the Ministry of Energy during 2010–2015 however this does not cover all households.

The issue of air pollution is also critical in ger areas and the capital city as a whole. Without proper emission control, household stoves remain a major source of air pollution and health risk because they can result in carbon monoxide poisoning inside gers. There is also serious urban air pollution in Ulaanbaatar during the winter season from vehicles as well as coal fired power stations, many of which are located close to the city and surrounding ger areas. With this context, it is necessary to understand how women and men experience and respond to energy-related changes.

---

[96]   ADB. 2013. *Technical Assistance Consultant's Report Mongolia: Updating the Energy Sector Development Plan*. Manila.

[97]   ADB. 2018. *Ulaanbaatar Air Quality Improvement Program: Report and Recommendation of the President (RRP MON 51199). Manila.*

[98]   Two of three coal-based CHP plants in Ulaanbaatar have operated for more than 45 years, and the largest plant coal-based CHP, has operated for more than 25 years, without proper emission control devices.

[99]   This information was in part obtained during the November 2019 consultant site visit to a local electricity distribution company, the Eastern Branch Office of the Ulaanbaatar Electricity Distribution Network, the Khoroo governments offices and a family home in a ger area. Ulaanbaatar, Bayanzurkh District, 21st Khoroo.

2.4.2 Gender Issues in the Energy Sector

Energy and access to energy sources can affect women and men differently. Women and girls in Mongolia are responsible for most of the household chores, and in rural areas, maintaining the upkeep of the fire used to heat the houses throughout the winters is a time consuming and onerous daily task, as well as cooking and cleaning. The short daylight hours in the winter make even simple tasks more difficult if the household does not have a reliable energy source. The ability to connect to the outside world for education and learning opportunities and emergency and/or health services requires a reliable and regular supply of energy. Even in peri-urban areas, access to energy can be limited and this limited access disproportionately affects women. Rural people often travel to urban centers for access to goods and services, and outside the capital city, these urban centers often face power outages due to grid overload. During these power outages, the extra time required to maintain heat in the house and prepare meals increases the workload of women.

A critical gender issue in the energy sector in Mongolia is the reliance on coal-based stoves and additional firewood for heating and cooking in the *ger* areas, which remains primarily the responsibility of women and girls. The health impacts of such "dirty" energy sources are disproportionately felt by women and girls. While there is little sex-disaggregated data in Mongolia on these impacts, evidence from around the world suggests that changes towards clean energy sources for household use can not only reap health benefits for women and girls but also free up time for them to pursue economic, educational, and personal activities.[100] While women are the primary users of energy in the home, in some cases they may also be the head of household and therefore the "consumer" of energy. It is therefore increasingly important that women participate in and are aware of energy policy decision making that affects them.

The energy sector worldwide is one of the least gender diverse economic sectors.[101] In Mongolia, approximately 75% of the energy workforce is male. There are few female leaders and decision makers, and cultural biases perpetuate gender inequalities. Although women in Mongolia are better educated than men on average, men generally hold more managerial positions than women across all sectors.[102] Yet this sector has the greatest possibilities for women's employment because of its multidisciplinary dimensions. Strategies are discussed in detail in a 2019 report on gender and renewable energy, and they include gender mainstreaming, tailored training and skills development, attracting and retaining talent through childcare support and part time and flexible hours, all of which would contribute to more women in decision making roles in the energy sector of Mongolia.[103]

2.4.3 Overview of Laws and Policies Related to the Energy Sector

The Law on Energy 2001 (Rev. 2015) is the umbrella law over a group of laws on energy. It regulates matters related to energy generation, transmission, distribution, dispatch and supply activities, construction of energy facilities, and energy consumption. It provides the process for licensing of entities involved in the energy chain, from generators of energy through to the suppliers and consumers. The law establishes the Energy Regulatory Agency which is responsible for regulating the tariffs for the supply of energy to consumers, whereas the Law on Renewable Energy regulates relationships and actions concerning the generation and use of renewable energy sources. It allows private independent power producers—generators—to build and operate facilities using renewable energy sources (solar, wind, hydropower, geothermal mill, and biomass that are not connected to the grid) to deliver the electricity to "transmission licensees" in listed districts. Thereafter, the electricity and/or heat is available to consumers, although this law does not cover the relationship with consumers.

100   UN Environment Programme. 2020. *Powering Equality: Women's Entrepreneurship Transforming Asia's Energy Sector.*
101   C. Tam. 2018. *Gender Diversity in Energy Sector Is Critical to Clean Energy Transition.* International Energy Agency.
102   A.D. Schmillen and N. Sandig. 2018. *Perceptions of Precariousness: A Qualitative Study of Constraints Underlying Gender Disparities in Mongolia's Labor Market.* Washington, DC. World Bank.
103   International Renewable Energy Agency. 2019. *Renewable Energy: A Gender Perspective.* Abu Dhabi.

The last law reviewed in this report was the Energy Conservation Law 2015 which is designed to provide for the efficient use and conservation of energy by designating state authorities, rights and obligations of consumers, and conservation services with penalties for violation. It provides for an Energy Conservation Council to work under the supervision of the Energy Regulatory Commission. The strategy is to conserve energy by providing energy more efficiently and changing consumer energy use habits and behaviors. It promotes the use of modern technology and equipment.

Within this complex scope of laws, several energy policies are also in place. The National Renewable Energy Program (2005–2020) was gender analyzed for this report as critical to building resilience and in line with the just transition to clean energy. A brief review of other policies including the State Policy on Energy 2015–2030, and the State Policy on Renewable Energy 2015–2030 showed a lack of any reference to gender equality and gender issues.

2.4.4 Gender Analysis Summary of Energy Laws and Policies

A gender analysis was conducted of laws and policies relevant to energy, particularly renewable energy (Table 5). The color coded system is used to categorize the laws and policies and demonstrates the state of gender mainstreaming as of 2021.

Table 5: Summary of Gender Inclusion in Energy Laws and Policies

Law/Policy	Summary of Gender References
Law on Energy 2001 (Rev. 2015)	There is a reference to "individuals" or "legal entities", but there is nothing in the legislation that suggests or promotes any role for women, even though they are involved in multiple ways in its implementation.
Law on Renewable Energy 2007 (Rev. 2015 and 2019)	The language used throughout is "person" or "legal entity" and there is nothing in the legislation that suggests or promotes any role for women. The prime persons affected by this policy are legal entities who are the generators and transmission licensees.
Energy Conversation Law 2015	There is no reference to gender equality or the rights of women or men concerning energy conservation, nor does the law explicitly link to the LPGE.
National Renewable Energy Program (2005–2020)	The policy fails to mention gender or gender issues and they relate to the promotion and adoption of renewable energy.

LPGE = Law on Promotion of Gender Equality.
Note: Color coding: gender responsive (green), gender sensitive (yellow), not yet gender mainstreamed (orange).
Source: Asian Development Bank.

Overall, energy laws and policies lack any reference to the essential concepts of equality and nondiscrimination, despite the significant impact and potential benefits energy access and energy consumption have for women in Mongolia. For example, women are *indirectly* affected by the implementation of the Law on Renewable Energy as consumers of the energy that is produced and transmitted and then becomes available to them in their households. As they are the primary users of energy in the home, women would benefit most from cleaner and more sustainable energy available to them. Yet the law and policy documents reviewed treat sector regulation as a purely technical matter and take no account of how the sector as a whole affects women and men differently. None of the laws or policies require gender analysis, collection of sex-disaggregated data, or gender mainstreaming. There is also no reference to the LPGE, which would support the provision and use of such tools to address gender inequalities in energy law and policy.

2.5 Strengthening the Socioeconomic Resilience of Women

Strengthening women's resilience requires more than developing and applying gender sensitized and responsive laws and policies that are specifically directed to climate change and disasters. As presented, these phenomena occur within existing social and economic structures, in which there are already different gender roles, as well as gender discrimination and inequalities that influence how disasters and climate change affect women and men.

This subsection focuses on a selection of national laws that build women's socioeconomic resilience as outlined in the *National Good Practice Legislative Framework on Women's Resilience to Climate Change and Disasters* (Figure 1). It includes laws preventing violence against women and girls, laws on land, inheritance, access to finance, education and training, and decent employment (formal and informal), among others. Given the enormous scope, the following three major themes were selected for their greatest immediate relevance to women's resilience to climate and disaster risk:

(i)   combating violence against women and girls;
(ii)   improving women's rights to assets; and
(iii) improving women's access to decent work.

These were all identified in the June 2018 *Ulaanbaatar Declaration*, adopted by the International Conference on Sustainable Development Goals: Gender and Development, as well as in CEDAW GR37.[104] The following subsections are presented as a discussion, not as summary tables similar to the previous sections because there is often only one law or policy covering each area or in some cases several laws some of which have already been discussed.

2.5.1 Combating Violence Against Women and Girls

Violence against women is a form of gender discrimination that reduces women's health and well-being, impacts their livelihoods through lost time in work or education, and increases their vulnerability to shocks. Overall, it inhibits women's social and economic capacity to reduce their risk, respond to and recover from disasters, adapt to climate change, and participate in emerging opportunities such as in the green economy. As of 2021, there was no reference to gender-based violence or violence against women in the context of disaster or climate change laws or policies in Mongolia. The most relevant national law on the topic is the Law to Combat Domestic Violence (Rev. 2016).

The objectives of the Law to Combat Domestic Violence (LCDV) are to establish the legal framework to detect and bring domestic violence to an end.[105] The LCDV refers to both male and female victims, children, and perpetrators. As women comprise the greatest number of victims of domestic violence, it is a law that—if implemented in a gender-responsive way with specific regard to the needs of women—is highly important to address domestic violence. Overall, it is a good practice law on the subject. However, common concerns about the implementation of the LCDV include insufficient protection; access to shelters and service centers, especially for women and girls with disabilities and women in remote rural areas;[106] underreporting to the police by victims and/or survivors;[107]

---

[104]   Government of Mongolia, Ministry of Labor and Social Protection and National Committee on Gender Equality. 2019. *Mongolia Gender Situational Analysis: Advances, Challenges and Lessons Learned since 2005*. Ulaanbaatar (under ADB's technical assistance financed by Japan Fund for Poverty Reduction (TA9201).

[105]   Parliament of Mongolia. 2016. *Law to Combat Domestic Violence 2005*. Ulaanbaatar.

[106]   CEDAW. 2018. *Concluding Observations on the Combined Eighth and Ninth Periodic Reports of Mongolia*. paras. 18, 19. New York.

[107]   Government of Mongolia, Ministry of Labor and Social Protection and National Committee on Gender Equality. 2019. *Mongolia Gender Situational Analysis: Advances, Challenges and Lessons Learned since 2005*. Ulaanbaatar.

a weak system for intersector collaboration; and the effectiveness of behavior-change training programs for perpetrators.[108]

These areas of particular concern are relevant to the discussion on strengthening women's resilience as often rural women and girls face significant disadvantages due to the absence of social protection schemes including access to essential services (which shelters and services centers are considered to be) both during and following disasters. Globally, women experiencing intersecting forms of discrimination—such as ethnic minorities or the disabled—lack physical access to services, and barriers to communication during and after disasters heighten their risk of violence.[109] The prevalence and nature of domestic violence in Mongolia points to the need to address this issue urgently and as part of this effort, data and evidence need to be gathered on the prevalence of violence against women in the context of disasters and climate change.

2.5.2 Improving Women's Rights to Assets

CEDAW GR37 notes that women—specifically rural and indigenous women involved in food and agricultural work—are directly affected by disasters and climate change. GR37 acknowledges that women make up the majority of global small and subsistence farmers, and a significant proportion is farmworkers. This means that—as a result of discriminatory laws and social norms—women often have limited access to secure land tenure. Moreover, the farmland women are allotted is often of inferior quality and more prone to flooding, erosion, or other adverse climatic events (footnote 121). Internationally, often women do not possess the legal and socially recognized landownership necessary to adapt to changing climatic conditions effectively (footnote 121). This includes not only the tenure of the land but also how women may inherit land or housing. Women's entrepreneurship can also be hindered by their limited land and property rights.[110]

Land tenure security provides greater certainty of access to land in the event of a disaster and underpins the ability of people to return to their livelihoods, food production, and rebuilding activities.[111] Land tenure is a critical issue for women and it has been said that "the question of land itself is a prism through which structural patterns of gender inequality can be revealed."[112] Land rights and land use are especially important to herders in Mongolia, yet a much lower proportion of herder women than men have household property registered in their names.[113] In addition, there are serious challenges to land productivity because of droughts, *dzuds,* and land degradation, leading to a shortage of pasture. This has led to disputes among and between herders, among crop growers and herders, and also between miners and residents. In these disputes, female heads of households are more vulnerable to losing their rights to land.[114]

In Mongolia, the LPGE requires government agencies to ensure that men and women have access to land on equal terms, and the Law on Land 2002 (revised in 2018) and the Law on Allocation of Land to Mongolian Citizens for

[108]   National Centre Against Violence and T. Altantsetseg. 2019. *The Implementation Context of Behaviour Change Program. Monitoring Report.* Ulaanbaatar.

[109]   CEDAW. 2018. *Gender Recommendation No. 37 on Gender-related dimensions of disaster risk reduction in the context of climate change.*

[110]   Government of Mongolia, Ministry of Labor and Social Protection and National Committee on Gender Equality. 2019. *Mongolia Gender Situational Analysis: Advances, Challenges and Lessons Learned since 2005.* Ulaanbaatar.

[111]   Government of Mongolia, NSO and ILO. 2019. *Accelerating the 2030 Sustainable Development Goals through Decent Work SDG Monitoring and Country Profile for Mongolia.* Ulaanbaatar.

[112]   The Global Initiative for Economic, Social and Cultural Rights. n.d. *Using CEDAW to Secure Women's Land and Property Rights - A Practical Guide.* Duluth, MN, USA.

[113]   SDC. 2015. *Gender analysis in pastoral livestock herding in Mongolia.* Ulaanbaatar, cited in: Government of Mongolia, Ministry of Labor and Social Protection and National Committee on Gender Equality. 2019. *Mongolia Gender Situational Analysis: Advances, Challenges and Lessons Learned since 2005.* Ulaanbaatar.

[114]   Government of Mongolia, Ministry of Labor and Social Protection and National Committee on Gender Equality. 2019. *Mongolia Gender Situational Analysis: Advances, Challenges and Lessons Learned since 2005.* Ulaanbaatar.

Ownership 2002 identify three main types of tenure: ownership, possession, and use.[115] The privatization process in 2002 permitted private citizens to own small plots of land for family residential purposes. It has been suggested that women did not fare well in the allocations of land under the 2002 Law. In particular, the quality and size of land allocated to women as plots were registered under the name of the male head of the household in 90% of the cases.[116] The 2018 NSO survey on asset ownership reports that 8% of men and 2% of women are reported owners of agricultural land and 6% of men and 1% of women are documented owners.[117] In response, a collaboration between several government and civil society organizations produced sex-disaggregated land information and data, in addition to training activities at national and subnational levels to improve the situation for women. As a result of the project financed by Millennium Challenge Corporation, the number of women with land registration increased among the target groups, from 35% to 41% in 2 years.[118]

Land security for women needs to improve in advance of further climate change and disasters. The key to this is ensuring that there is sufficient and relevant sex-disaggregated land information and data to enable targeted approaches to promote women's land rights. This needs to include not only quantitative but qualitative information, as the registration of women on land may also be connected to the stereotyping of women's roles.

Inheritance rights and housing are other key areas that are vital for women as they are connected to poverty and inextricably linked with economic autonomy. These rights are highly important to strengthening women's economic resilience to disasters and climate change. While almost two-thirds of Mongolian men own their own homes, only one-third of women do, and the proportion of registered ownership is lower still (men 55%, women 27%). Official registration of homeownership for women is also significantly lower in rural than in urban areas.[119]

The 2019 gender situational analysis of Mongolia points to these inequalities of ownership and inheritance of land—and other property and economic resources—and noted a remaining gap in quantitative data in this area (footnote 131). A survey undertaken in 2013 of 8,000 urban and rural respondents showed that the female share in land inheritance was only 27.2%. Moreover, the tradition of passing land and other immovable property down to sons is still strong. In a 2014 survey, 72.4% of participants said that they would give their *khashaa* (fenced land) to their sons and only 17.6% planned to transfer the title deeds to their daughters (footnote 131, p. 20).

Inheritance law and practice is a source of serious discrimination against women, who often inherit a smaller share of property from their husband or father compared with widowers and sons.[120] In some instances, women are granted limited and controlled rights, such as receiving income only from the property of the deceased. Inequalities in inheritance rights and housing in Mongolia pose a compounding concern in the pursuit of strengthening women's resilience.

---

[115] Government of Mongolia, Ministry of Labor and Social Protection. 2011. *National Program on Gender Equality and Its Action Plan, Art. 9.2.* Ulaanbaatar.

[116] B. Robinson and A. Solongo. 2000. *The Gender Dimension of Economic Transition in Mongolia*: in The Mongolian Economy: A Manual of Applied Economics for a Country in Transition, pp. 231–255. Leicestershire, UK.

[117] Government of Mongolia, NSO. 2018. *Asset Ownership and Entrepreneurship from a Gender Perspective Pilot study report (in original language).* Ulaanbaatar.

[118] Government of Mongolia, Ministry of Labor and Social Protection and National Committee on Gender Equality. 2019. *Mongolia Gender Situational Analysis: Advances, Challenges and Lessons Learned since 2005.* p. 21. Ulaanbaatar.

[119] Government of Mongolia, Ministry of Labor and Social Protection and National Committee on Gender Equality. 2019. *Mongolia Gender Situational Analysis: Advances, Challenges and Lessons Learned since 2005.* Ulaanbaatar.

[120] The Global Initiative for Economic, Social and Cultural Rights. n.d. *Using CEDAW to Secure Women's Land and Property Rights - A Practical Guide.* Duluth, MN, USA.

2.5.3 General improvement of decent work for women

The final socioeconomic area covered in this report is that of decent work. As defined by the International Labour Organization (ILO), decent work encompasses "opportunities for work that is productive and delivers a fair income, security in the workplace and social protection for families, better prospects for personal development and social integration, freedom for people to express their concerns, organize and participate in the decisions that affect their lives and equality of opportunity and treatment for all women and men."[121] The key issues selected for this report that affect decent work for women in Mongolia are sexual harassment and discrimination in employment, and lower remuneration compared to men doing work of the same value. These issues impact the ability of women to gain and remain in decent work, and to build the economic security to manage shocks caused by climate change and disasters.

Workplace sexual harassment is a form of human rights violation[122] and gender-based violence.[123] As noted in the country profile, in Mongolia most victims of workplace sexual harassment are women, and perpetrators are overwhelmingly men with higher education, the majority of whom are senior managers.[124] As of 2021, some laws in Mongolia address sexual harassment in the workplace, including the LPGE and the Law on Infringement approved in 2020.[125] Historically, sexual harassment was reflected in the Criminal Code but was removed in 2017 (footnote 137). This created a void to remedy sexual harassment because thereafter it was not possible to order payment of fines, or compensation for damages due to sexual harassment. There has been discussion since 2018 about a potential revision of the Labor Code to include a provision on sexual harassment. An indication of the potential content of the provision (footnote 137, p. 62) has been set out in a 2020 report.[126] These positive trends are promising, and more can be done to promote implementation, such as through the development of guidelines and practical materials on preventing harassment in the workplace. Further, it is important to look beyond traditional workplaces and to other sectors such as health, education, and public transport to ensure that all workplaces and public spaces are free from harassment.

Women in Mongolia continue to receive lower wages than men in many sectors of the economy.[127] In 2018, women earned 82.1% of the average monthly remuneration of men. This is almost a 20% wage gap.[128] The disparity is greater for women in rural areas than in urban.[129] As of March 2019, the NSO stated that the gender pay gap in the country had increased to over 25%.[130] The widest gender pay gaps are found in manufacturing, construction, information and communications, finance, and insurance.[131] The LPGE refers to "equal pay for equal work and equal working conditions" (Article 11.3.4) however the concept of the ILO Convention—which Mongolia has ratified—is different.

---

[121] ILO. 2021. *Decent work.*

[122] CEDAW. 1989. *General Recommendation No. 12: Violence against Women - Eighth Session.*

[123] CEDAW. 1992. *General Recommendation No. 19: Violence against Women.*

[124] Government of Mongolia, Ministry of Labor and Social Protection and National Committee on Gender Equality. 2019. *Mongolia Gender Situational Analysis: Advances, Challenges and Lessons Learned since 2005.* p. 62. Ulaanbaatar.

[125] Government of Mongolia. 2020. *Law of Infringement 2020.* Article 6.26 states: (i) A person shall be fined one thousand units of togrog (Mongolian currency unit) or shall be punishable by imprisonment for a term of seven to thirty days and subjected to compulsory training if he or she expresses verbally, physically or by other means to engage in sexual acts with others which imposes work, position, honor, fame, property or emotional consequences to others. (ii) If an employer fails to fulfill its obligation to include in the internal labor regulations the norms for prevention of sexual harassment in the workplace and settlement of complaints, a legal entity shall be fined in the amount of one thousand five hundred units of *togrog.*

[126] There is now a new Labour Law of Mongolia 2020 that includes articles that prohibit harassment and sexual harassment in the workplace with reference to obligations and responsibilities of employers. It is not comprehensive and requires reference to other laws including LPGE for its comprehension and implementation.

[127] Government of Mongolia, NSO and ILO. 2019. *Accelerating the 2030 Sustainable Development Goals through Decent Work SDG Monitoring and Country Profile for Mongolia.* Ulaanbaatar.

[128] Government of Mongolia, Ministry of Labor and Social Protection. 2019. *Mongolia Comprehensive National-Level Review: Responses to questionnaire on implementation of the Beijing Declaration and Platform for Action.* p 7. Ulaanbaatar.

[129] Green Climate Fund. 2019. *Country Programme Mongolia.*

[130] Xinhua news. 2019. *Women in Mongolia Earn Less than Men.*

[131] Committee of Experts on the Application of Conventions and Recommendations, ILO. 2020. *Mongolia: Direct Request CEACR - Adopted 2019: Equal Remuneration Convention.* Geneva.

The convention does not refer only to "equal work" (being the same work) or to "equal working conditions" (being the same working conditions). Instead, the ILO requirement is to ensure equal remuneration for work or working conditions that may be quite different, but of "equal value." Work of "equal value" may be as different as heavy lifting in factory work (often done by men), to dexterity in inserting parts into machines in a factory (often done by women). This is an important distinction and is frequently the cause of gender wage gaps, as noted by CEDAW.[132]

Other compounding issues facing access for women to decent work in Mongolia include (i) the discrimination that occurs against women of reproductive age in recruitment and employment and career promotion opportunities; (ii) the effect of the triple burden of productive and reproductive roles with unpaid care work and the earlier retirement age (55 years for women and 60 years for men); and (iii) the ability to access minimum wage. There is "compelling international evidence" that minimum wages reduce overall inequality by raising pay at the bottom of the distribution relative to the middle and setting national minimum wages reduces inequality or wages and remuneration between women and men.[133] This is because women tend to be at the bottom end of income distribution, so a minimum wage sets a wage floor that improves wages for women.[134] Households headed by women make up over 10% of all households, and 43.8% of them are poor.[135] A minimum wage floor can also be extended to specific categories of work, in particular, work where women are disproportionately represented, as outlined by the ILO Committee of Experts on the Application of Conventions and Recommendations (CEACR) in its Direct Request to Mongolia in 2019.[136] The topic of minimum wages was also highlighted in the Ulaanbaatar Declaration of 2018 on the SDGs.[137]

Decent work includes important ingredients for strengthening the economic resilience of women to climate change and disasters; increasing the participation of women in the workforce; improving the types of jobs they perform; and their remuneration for those jobs. Agriculture, forestry (including fisheries and hunting), and light industry remain both the greatest source of employment for men and women in Mongolia, and are severely impacted by climate change and disasters. Decent work for women in agriculture, forestry (including fisheries and hunting), and light industry is, therefore, an important aspect of women's socioeconomic resilience in Mongolia. Effective implementation of the Food, Agriculture, and Light Industry Sector Gender Responsive Policy (2018–2025), with its analysis and priorities according to employment trends, will be a significant contribution for women to access decent work and the ability to build resilience to climate change and disasters.[138]

132   CEDAW. 2018. *Concluding Observations on the Combined Eighth and Ninth Periodic Reports of Mongolia*. New York.
133   J. Healy. 2009. *The Wages Safety Net of the Australian Industrial Relations Commission, 1993–2005*. Adelaide, Australia.
134   J. Romeyn et al. 2011. *Review of Equal Remuneration Principles*. Canberra, Australia.
135   Green Climate Fund. 2019. *Country Programme Mongolia*.
136   Committee of Experts on the Application of Conventions and Recommendations, ILO. 2020. *Mongolia: Direct Request CEACR - Adopted 2019: Equal Remuneration Convention*. Geneva.
137   Government of Mongolia. 2018. *Sustainable Development Goals: Gender and Development International Conference: Ulaanbaatar Declaration*. 28 June. Ulaanbaatar.
138   Government of Mongolia, Ministry of Food, Agriculture and Light Industry. 2018. *The Food, Agriculture and Light Industry Sector Gender-Responsive Policy (2018–2025)*. Ulaanbaatar.

3 Conclusion and Recommendations

The purpose of this report was to conduct a gender analysis of the national legal and policy frameworks of Mongolia to determine if laws, policies, and strategies consider gender inequalities in climate and disaster risk and contribute to strengthening women's resilience. The analysis found that the LPGE is an international best practice law on promoting gender equality and within it exists provisions for sector laws and policies to integrate gender equality principles. However, as of 2021, there is limited adoption and translation of the LPGE in key sector laws and policies. Laws and policies that affect women's resilience to climate change and disasters in Mongolia are not yet gender mainstreamed. There are two exceptions. The NAPCC is classified as gender sensitive due to its mention of gender equality as an implementation principle, and its reference to promoting the participation of women in international and regional activities related to climate change. The Environmental Sector Gender Strategy stands out as the gender responsive policy that directly promotes strengthening women's resilience. Yet, without a suite of policy initiatives—as well as corresponding legislation to enforce commitments to gender equality—it is unclear how effective the NAPCC and the sector strategy will be in strengthening women's resilience.

Overall, a notable characteristic of legislation in Mongolia is that it routinely provides for formal equality between men and women (equal treatment of women and men). The modernized laws do not distinguish between the sexes except for specific and clear biological sex-based reasons such as reproductive health, maternity, and motherhood. Indeed, many of the laws (and policies) reviewed for this report make no mention of men or women or gender at all. The underlying assumption is that, if a law applies to everyone, then women and men should always be treated the same under that law. The result is that many of the laws do not recognize or address the different roles, responsibilities, social, cultural, economic, and political contexts and backgrounds of women and girls or men and boys. To rectify this, the LPGE needs to be leveraged and comprehensive disaggregated data need to be collected, analyzed, and used to form the evidence base for decision making, ensuring equality of outcome for women and men in areas that affect resilience.

CEDAW GR37 articulates a push for policy coherence and effective integration of gender equality within legislation and policies in sectors relevant to climate change and disaster risk. The framework developed for this report has provided an approach to identify laws and policies that impact the ability of women to build resilience to climate change and disasters. The gender scale adopted in the analysis is an important tool to understand across multiple sectors where gender has or has not yet been mainstreamed. Based on the results of this analysis, a series of recommendations have been made, both specific and general.

Specific Recommendations

(i) **Develop an Emergency Management Gender Strategy.** It is recommended that NEMA work with the NCGE to begin developing a gender strategy following the LPGE as soon as possible.

(ii) **Review the National Programme of Community Participatory Disaster Risk Reduction (2015–2025).** It is recommended that the government review the policy implementation. This could draw on research and analysis undertaken in developing a gender strategy, and include consultations with women and men in communities to determine the best way to introduce gender analysis and a balanced representation of women and men in numbers and decision-making roles in community disaster risk reduction.

(iii) **Develop regulations under the Law on Environmental Protection and the EIA Law to increase the gender responsiveness of public participation in environmental policy.** The government could utilize the LEP and EIA Law powers to make regulations on public participation and community consultations on environmental protection and approval of new projects or activities, to require that the consultation procedures and environmental management plans are gender sensitive, and to provide clear guidance on how this is done. This can provide a standard for community and public participation that can be implemented at multiple levels and work towards increasing the voice of women—and other groups who are sometimes marginalized—especially those in rural areas.

(iv) **Develop an Energy Gender Responsive Policy.** The gender analysis conducted in this report demonstrates that gender is yet to be mainstreamed into energy laws and policies. An overall recommendation is to mainstream gender considerations into each energy law and policy and any action plans which may be relevant to them. This could commence with the development of a gender responsive policy for energy to be undertaken by the Ministry of Energy with the assistance of NCGE.

General Recommendations

(i) **Collection and analysis of disaggregated data (by sex and other indicators) needs to be prioritized.** Noted as the first specific measure under CEDAW GR37, the collection and assessment of disaggregated data are critical to understanding the complex impacts of climate change and disaster risk. This report has demonstrated that as of 2021, there is little disaggregated data and evidence to identify gender-based vulnerabilities in Mongolia. Collection of data disaggregated by sex, age disability, ethnicity, and geographical location at the minimum is recommended. Given the recent memorandum of understanding signed between the National Committee on Gender Equality and the National Statistics Office—and commitment to improving gender statistics collection and use in Mongolia—an opportunity to focus on gender and climate change and disaster related statistics exists.

(ii) **Increasing the participation of women in environmental, climate change, and disaster risk management decision making is essential.** As of 2021, women have very little say over the policy formulation process due to the limited number of women in decision-making positions and a lack of mandate for gender-inclusive processes. The LPGE stipulates specific provisions for increasing the participation of women, including in the civil service. Targeting sectors—such as energy—is key to strengthening the resilience of women to climate change and disasters.

(iii) **Consolidate a gender responsive approach to climate change and disaster risk.** It is recommended that the MET and NEMA work in close collaboration with the NCGE to ensure that (a) all national policy processes, international compliance reports and international climate finance proposals—specifically the new national action plan and the implementation of the Green Climate Fund country program—routinely include the achievement of gender equality as a key strategic objective; (b) the NCGE becomes a permanent part of the institutional structure for national environmental, climate change and disaster risk management policymaking at the highest level, and the sector gender councils are integrated within the MET and NEMA processes; (c) there is provision for a minimum proportion of women or men on all national and subnational implementation committees and policymaking bodies; (d) the goals and objectives of the environmental gender strategy—and other gender strategies as developed—are integrated into the policy process; and (e) the policies include budget, gender indicators and monitoring in line with the SDGs as a whole, and especially SDG5 on gender equality and empowerment of women and girls.

Glossary

Discrimination against girls and women: Any distinction, exclusion, or restriction made on the basis of sex which has the effect or purpose of impairing or nullifying the recognition, enjoyment, or exercise by women irrespective of their marital status, on the basis of equality of men and women, of human rights and fundamental freedoms in the political, economic, social, cultural civil or any other field. The definition includes not just **direct discrimination** (or intentional discrimination), but any act that has the effect of creating or perpetuating inequality between men and women which may be **indirect discrimination.**

Source: United Nations Entity for Gender Equality and the Empowerment of Women (UN Women). 2017. *Gender Equality Glossary.*

Gender: Refers to the roles, behaviors, activities, and attributes that a given society at a given time considers appropriate for men and women. In addition to the social attributes and opportunities associated with being male and female and the relationships between women and men and girls and boys, gender also refers to the relations between women and those between men. These attributes, opportunities, and relationships are socially constructed and are learned through socialization processes. They are context/time-specific and changeable. Gender determines what is expected, allowed, and valued in a woman or a man in a given context. In most societies, there are differences and inequalities between women and men in responsibilities assigned, activities undertaken, access to, and control over resources, as well as decision-making opportunities. Gender is part of the broader sociocultural context, as are other important criteria for sociocultural analysis including class, race, poverty level, ethnic group, sexual orientation, age, etc. (see discrimination above).

Source: UN Women. 2017. *Gender Equality Glossary.*

Gender analysis: An examination of how differences in gender roles, activities, needs, opportunities and rights/ entitlements affect men, women, girls, and boys in certain situations or contexts. Gender analysis examines the relationships between females and males and their access to and control of resources and the constraints they face relative to each other. A gender analysis should be integrated into all sector assessments or situational analyses to ensure that gender-based injustices and inequalities are not exacerbated by interventions and that where possible, greater equality and justice in gender relations are promoted.

Source: UN Women. 2017. *Gender Equality Glossary.*

Gender equality: Refers to the equal rights, responsibilities, and opportunities of women and men and girls and boys. Equality does not mean that women and men will become the same but that women's and men's rights, responsibilities, and opportunities will not depend on whether they are born male or female. Gender equality implies that the interests, needs, and priorities of both women and men are taken into consideration, recognizing the diversity of different groups of women and men. Gender equality is not a women's issue but should concern and engage men as well as women. Equality between women and men is seen both as a human rights issue and as a precondition for, and indicator of, sustainable people-centered development.

Source: UN Women. 2017. *Gender Equality Glossary.* Gender equality includes not only **formal equality** (de jure equality – treating men and women the same) but also includes **substantive equality** (de facto equality – equality of outcome in fact for both women and men); CEDAW. 2004. *General Recommendations adopted by the Committee on the Elimination of Discrimination Against Women. General Recommendation No. 25.*

Gender mainstreaming: Gender mainstreaming is the chosen approach of the United Nations system and international community toward realizing progress on the rights of women and girls, as a subset of human rights to which the United Nations dedicates itself. It is not a goal or objective on its own. Mainstreaming a gender perspective is the process of assessing the implications for women and men of any planned action, including legislation, policies, or programs, in all areas and at all levels. It is a way to make concerns and experiences of women—as well as men—an integral dimension of the design, implementation, monitoring, and evaluation of policies and programs in all political, economic, and societal spheres so that women and men benefit equally and inequality is not perpetuated. The ultimate goal is to achieve gender equality.

Source: UN Women. 2017. *Gender Equality Glossary.*

Gender negative: Applies gender norms, roles, and stereotypes that reinforce gender inequalities.

Source: UN Women. 2017. *Gender Equality Glossary.*

Gender neutral: Gender is not considered relevant to outcomes.

Source: UN Women. 2017. *Gender Equality Glossary.*

Gender positive/transformative: Changes gender norms, roles, and transforms unequal gender relations to promote shared power, control of resources, decision-making, and support for women's empowerment.

Source: UN Women. 2017. *Gender Equality Glossary.*

Gender sensitive: Considers gender norms, roles, and relations taking into account sociocultural factors, but does not actively address gender inequalities.

Source: World Health Organization (WHO). 2012. https://www.who.int/globalchange/publications/Mainstreaming_Gender_Climate.pdf.

Gender responsive: Pays attention to specific needs of women and men and intentionally uses gender considerations to affect the design, implementation, and results of legislation, policies, and programs.

Source: UNICEF. 2017. *Gender Equality Glossary of Terms and Concepts.*